MOTORCYCLES, MERLINS
AND MOSQUITOS

PETER McMANUS

MOTORCYCLES, MERLINS AND MOSQUITOS

The Story of Chris Harrison, Racing Motorcyclist,
Rolls-Royce Engineer, Mosquito Pilot

breedon **books**
PUBLISHING

First published in Great Britain in 2009 by The Breedon Books Publishing
Company Limited, Breedon House, 3 The Parker Centre, Derby, DE21 4SZ

BY THE SAME AUTHOR

ONE MAN'S MOTORCYCLES 1939-1949
Boyhood in Rhyl, North Wales, engineering apprenticeship in Dickensian
conditions in Derby, aero-engine development at Rolls-Royce then starting in the
motorcycle business buying, selling, repairing, restoring and racing motorcycles of
the 1920s and 30s. £14.95. Softback.

ONE MAN'S SCOTLAND
Deerstalking from the earliest days and our own 40 years' experience. Over 50
photographs from stalker, author and naturalist Lea MacNally.
£16.95. Softback. £29.95 signed, numbered, limited edition hardback.

ONE MAN'S GUN QUEST
My 50 Year search for fine English guns and rifles.
With photographs by Ernest Drury Smith and the Birmingham gun trade.
£24.95. Hardback.

RICHTHOFEN JAGDSTAFFEL AHEAD
In 1917, 40 Squadron, Royal Flying Corps, faced Richthofen's deadly Jagdstaffel 11
on the Western Front in France. One of the pilots was Lionel Blaxland and his five
photograph albums of the pilots and planes of those days together with his Flying
Log Book were made available to write his story. In addition to the Blaxland
photographs there are many illustrations by one of the world's leading aviation
artists and historians, John Batchelor.
£20. Hardback.

All books are written to the same formula: short chapters and lots of illustrations.
The 'One Man's' trilogy takes a light-hearted look at the whole scene.

All available post free and signed on request from:
MEP Publishing, Newton Park Farm, Newton Solney, Burton on Trent, DE15 0SS.

Editor: Ross McManus
Cutaway painting of Merlin II engine on page 139: John Batchelor
Typesetting and artwork by David Billings, M.P. Bio Science,
Harrison Court, Hilton, Derbyshire.

ISBN 978-1-85983-766-5
Printed and bound by Gutenberg Press Ltd, Malta.

THIS BOOK IS NOT ONLY A TRIBUTE TO CHRIS HARRISON BUT ALSO TO ALL THE BRAVE MEN WHO FLEW IN WORLD WAR TWO.

TO MY FAMILY WHO HAVE SUPPORTED MY WRITING EFFORTS AND, AS ALWAYS, MY GRANDSONS ADAM AND CLIVE.

ABOUT THIS BOOK

This book tells the story of Chris Harrison, a remarkable man. A lifelong motorcycle enthusiast, he was, and still is at the age of 94, a brilliant engineer who gave sterling service at Rolls-Royce. He was my boss in my Rolls-Royce days, and we have never lost touch. I knew practically every one of Chris's motorcycling friends who are featured in this book. As well as being an engineer, Chris was also one of those brave men who flew as night-fighter pilots through the war-torn skies of occupied Europe.

When I told my son, Ross, that the book was finally written he said 'Is Harrison Court mentioned?' When I replied 'No,' his wife, Remila, immediately said 'Then the book is not finished!' So let me explain about Harrison Court. Ross moved his business to Hilton, South Derbyshire, buying two large, newly built factory units in the St Modwen's Business Park. They are situated in a T-shaped court which, up to then, had not been named. Ross suggested 'Harrison Court' so that Chris's name would live on. This was accepted, and anyone who enquires about the origin of the name will be told about Chris Harrison.

My thanks to everyone involved:
Chris Harrison for his many letters and conversations on which the book is based.

My family and especially Edna, who did the scanning, who had to put up with me writing the book. Ross and Dave, who have gone to endless trouble on their computers. The world's leading authority on Velocettes, Derbyshire's Ivan Rhodes, who supplied all the Velocette photographs. John Batchelor, one of the world's leading aviation artists, who very kindly allowed me to use his painting of the Mosquito cockpit and some of the paintings of aircraft. Motorcycle racer John Cooper, who provided the McEvoy photographs. Tom Cushing, owner of the Little Snoring airfield, for many of the Little Snoring photographs. A number of the motorcycle photographs are by Eric E. Thompson. Anna Seddon of Littleover Library, Derby, who went to endless trouble to find long out-of-print books essential for this and all my previous books. Finally, all those who have helped with advice and illustrations.

The painting of a Mosquito cockpit is from Mosquito info Guide No. 1. The illustrations are by one of the world's leading aviation artists, John Batchelor.

CONTENTS

'IN THE EARLY DAYS OF THE WAR
THE FATE OF ENGLAND AND THE
WORLD DEPENDED QUITE
LITERALLY ON THE EFFORTS OF THE
MEN AT DERBY.'

Historian Ian Lloyd.

Chris Harrison was one of those men.

Chapter 1

MEETING CHRIS HARRISON

At the end of the war, having served my engineering apprenticeship at George Fletcher and Company of Derby, working on all kinds of war work, I applied to Rolls-Royce for a job on their technical staff. I was taken on and initially worked on Merlin development under Tony Neaverson. Not long afterwards, I was transferred to the test-beds at Sinfin to work in the test office with a team of highly talented engineers. All of them were perfectly happy to pass on the benefit of their experience, and many were motorcyclists or had been motorcyclists.

The head of the test office was Joe Capel, and my immediate boss was Chris Harrison. In charge of the whole operation was Ernest Eltis, a man with a brilliant brain who was a refugee from Germany. He was only a young man, but that was no barrier at Rolls-Royce. Talent and ability were what mattered. Ernest went on to become an engineering director of Rolls-Royce.

The Rolls-Royce Merlin and Griffon engines were run on all kinds of tests, and it was our job to analyse the performance and solve any problems that might occur. It was stimulating work.

Chris was an old motorcyclist so we got on very well indeed. He was a very fair boss, and if he did find it necessary to reprimand you it was done politely, firmly and with no trace of small-mindedness. When I later became an employer, I would often reflect on how Chris would have handled a particular situation.

Chris was an engineer to his fingertips, but he was not only merely a practical engineer but also a brilliant design engineer. We would encounter a

Handsome young Chris Harrison during his flying training at Miami, Oklahoma, 1941.

Chris at Donington in 1938 with his friend and racing mechanic Joe Hoult. An Excelsior Manxman is behind the Norton. Note the ancient overhead camshaft Velocette in the foreground, which was not competing.

problem that appeared to be insoluble and would baffle everyone in the test office. Chris, however, would get his brains into top gear and invariably come up with a solution. Having done so, some people would say 'I could have thought of that', but they *hadn't* thought of it; Chris had.

Chris was never afraid to call a spade a spade. This did him no harm at Sinfin, where he was universally liked by everyone, not just in the test office but throughout the plant. There are times, however, when calling a spade a spade is not the diplomatic way forward, and later on in life Chris was to learn this from bitter experience. Harry Swift, a former Rolls-Royce works manager, knew Chris and got on very well with him, but he once said to him 'Remember, Chris, you can kill someone just as effectively with a rapier as with a sabre'.

Chris went on to run the test office, and his career continued to progress. In 1953 Rolls-Royce decided to open a factory in Australia to service the Australian Air Force Rolls-Royce Dart turbo-props using Chris's design for turbo-prop testing. Alec Harvey-Bailey was the son of one of Henry Royce's original engineers and a fine designer. Alec was chosen to run the Australian operation. Chris got on well with him and was asked to move to Australia to work on the new project.

About two years ago Chris wrote his autobiography, and I had it published for him in England. It is very much an engineer's book with much technical detail. Chris wrote in detail about the triumphs and disasters of his Australian years in this autobiography, so I will restrict myself to a bare outline of that period in Chris's career. Originally Chris got on very well at Rolls-Royce in Australia, but eventually his determination to call a spade a spade did not suit Harvey-Bailey, and their relationship deteriorated badly. Eventually Harvey-Bailey found a pretext on which to dismiss Chris, and he was out on his own in Australia. With hindsight, it would probably have been better for him to have left Australia then and returned to Rolls-Royce in Derby, but as his home was now in Australia he decided to stay on. The next few years were very difficult indeed for him as the working relationship at Rolls-Royce became an issue when he was applying for other jobs. He finally worked for Goodyear in their aviation tyres division. He was once again able to demonstrate his engineering ability and his flair for solving problems.

Sadly his beloved wife, Madge, died a few years ago. Chris is now 94 years old and still in reasonable health. He rode motorcycles until he was 90, still drives a car and still works on vintage motorcycles.

Chapter 2

CHRIS'S GENEROUS GESTURE

One morning my wife Edna was opening the post. 'What are you and Chris up to?' she asked. 'We're not up to anything,' I replied. 'Then what is this bill?' she demanded.

As soon as I saw it, I knew what it was all about. It was an invoice for the cost of transporting a vintage motorcycle from the Port of Felixtowe to our home in South Derbyshire.

At that time Chris was in his mid-80s, and two or three years beforehand he had discovered a long disused saw-bench near his home in Australia. It was driven by a partially dismantled 1923 600cc Douglas twin motorcycle. The drive was by chain from engine to gearbox, then vee belt to the rear wheel. The wheels had been thrown away, as had the front forks. The rear frame tubes had been sawn off and a piece of iron gas piping substituted for the handlebars. Chris resolved to rebuild the machine from these un-promising remains.

But what a task! Suitable wheels were found, but where do you find front forks for a 1923 Douglas? Chris drew a blank, but I happened to meet a local motorcycle enthusiast who had been looking for a set of forks for a mid-1930s AJS and had eventually found a suitable set at an autojumble. On the stall was a set of forks that no one had been able to identify and had remained unsold. From his description I realised that these were the forks Chris needed. I got in touch with the stallholder and bought them on Chris's behalf, packed them up and sent them to Chris.

Chris made replacement rear-frame tubes and the missing carrier. Originally the carrier held a pair of metal toolboxes with opening leather fronts. Chris made them all. He also made a replica of the original sweeping cow-horn handlebars, as well as lots of other work: front and rear brake systems, footboards and fittings, chaincases and more.

Next, the engine. For valves he searched a local scrapyard and found that valves from a Japanese car engine were just slightly larger and so ideal for the job, and subsequently the engine was successfully rebuilt. All the nickel plating was done on his own home-made nickel plating set, suitable mudguards were fitted and then he re-sprayed the whole machine. Finally the great moment arrived when all the work had been completed, and all that remained was to see if it would fire up. It started and ran beautifully.

Having done all this, he made a steel-framed packing case for it and, without a word to us, shipped it to us as a gift! It is the most generous gift we have ever received in our life in the world of motorcycles.

The 1923 600cc Douglas that Chris Harrison rebuilt from a wreck and then shipped to the McManus family as a gift. A small brass plaque on the top of the front forks reads:
'Chris Harrison 1914 – Donington rider, Mosquito pilot, Rolls-Royce engineer
Restored and rode this
1923 600cc Douglas in Australia 1996/99'

This photograph, taken at Brooklands in 1920, surely invokes the very spirit of the 1920s. The war is over, happy days are here again and anything goes! Miss Rita Don, sister of racing man Kaye Don, is on her Zenith, with its Gradua Gear. The coffee grinder handle opened and closed the drive pulley, at the same time moving the rear wheel to keep constant belt tension. This gave a limited range of gear ratios denied to contemporary single-geared belt drivers. Mrs H.S. Powell on right has a two-stroke Metro Tyler. After a day's riding these Bright Young Things would don their outrageously short skirts and dance the night away!

I then rang the office at Felixtowe to be told that before the machine could be dispatched VAT would have to be paid, albeit at a reduced rate, so I got in touch with the vintage motorcycle expert Mike Worthington-Williams. 'The VAT people,' he said 'know nothing about vintage motorcycles, but they have an uncanny sixth sense, so if you undervalue a machine they will know and you will be guilty of attempting to defraud the Revenue'. So we decided on a value of £5,000.

The great moment came when the machine eventually arrived and we were delighted with it.

It was all typical of Chris Harrison.

Chapter 3

IN THE BEGINNING

Chris Harrison was born in October 1914 in Watford. He was always fascinated by speed. His father was an architect and surveyor with one of the British railway companies, and as a result the family frequently travelled on trains. Chris would always be in the corridor with his head stuck out of the window, regardless of the fact that he frequently got bits of grit from the engine smoke in his eyes, but the feeling of the wind in his face and the sensation of speed always drew him back to the window.

He vividly remembers when he was very young riding in a charabanc over the Yorkshire Moors and being allowed to sit next to the driver. He was fascinated by the sound of the engine, the grinding of the transmission and watching the speedometer needle which wobbled around furiously, but he was highly excited when they were actually doing over an amazing 30mph.

He was conscious of motorcycles by about 1924, when he was nine years of age going on 10. He remembers seeing one of the earliest motorcycles, which was started by pedalling it along the road and which required LPA (light pedal assistance) on hills. He can also remember the inlet-over-exhaust-valve Rudge Whitworths which had a hole in the tank above the inlet valve. Chris and his pals always said this was for safety's sake so that if the valve blew out it did not make a hole in the petrol tank! He never really knew what the hole was for, but that is what they always believed. He can also remember seeing a Zenith Gradua. They were belt driven and had no gearbox, but the pulley on the engine shaft was expanded and contracted by a coffee grinder handle on the petrol tank. This allowed a rudimentary range of gears as the belt rode

The beautifully proportioned 3hp Clarendon of 1903–04. LPA (light pedal assistance) would be required on steep hills.

higher or lower on the engine shaft pulley. To maintain constant belt tension the handle moved the rear-wheel spindle forward and backward in unison.

One of the local motorcyclists had a tremendous stammer, which was really painful to listen to. Chris and his pals used to stand next to him trying to guess what his next world would be. When he got it right he would point and try another few words. He had a Triumph with gears like an oversized three-speed bicycle hub, which seemed to work. When he was flying along at 40mph, however, he could address the pillion rider without a trace of stammer.

Chris also remembers being on the side of the road and seeing people clearing up where a man named Fox on a very smart looking P&M Panther had sadly just killed himself. He had attempted to take a corner too fast and hit a telegraph pole, so Chris was well aware that motorcycles could be dangerous.

Chris's elder brother, who ultimately became chairman of the London Press Club, was a cub reporter in the mid-1920s, and Chris well remembers the Royal Enfield inlet-over-exhaust-valve V-twin that he rode. It had a round glass oil tank under the saddle which you could no longer see into to check the oil level as it was covered in sludge. Amazingly, for those days, it had a dry-sump engine and it must have been one of the earliest examples. He later had a side-valve BSA, then an overhead valve model, both flat tankers. On one journey he ran into a hole in the road where the road was being repaired. It was dark but no one had put any warning lights against it. This ended his motorcycling career in about 1928.

The local Watford motorcycle club was quite a thriving concern, and they used to stage grass-track races. Chris and his pals would walk a few miles to see the race meetings, and he does not remember ever having to pay to get in. The entry fee was about sixpence, but 10-year-olds got in free. One of the famous riders he remembers seeing was Fay Taylour, who also in the late 1920s rode in the new sport of speedway. She emigrated to Australia in 1954 and had a second-hand car business in Sydney, but to Chris's regret he never got in touch with her.

Another successful rider Chris encountered was George Wilkes. It took a very good rider to beat George. Chris also remembers Doug Pirie, who won the 1934 Senior Manx Grand Prix. In those grass-track days, George rode a 350cc ohv BSA, and at one meeting Chris was lying on the grass

A 1913 500cc Triumph with a three-speed hub in the rear wheel, rather like a big three-speed hub fitted to a bicycle. Handle with care!

Another delightful design which was ahead of its time. This 1914 TT Royal Enfield had dry-sump lubrication compared to the usual total-loss systems of that era. 350cc V-twin, inlet-over-exhaust valves and a glass oil tank. Eight were entered in the 1914 TT and, in a remarkable display of reliability, all finished. F.J. Walker was third but, sadly, crashed into a barrier beyond the finish line and was killed.

when George came and spoke to a spectator who was standing near Chris and his mate. They amused themselves by writing their names on the toecap of his riding boot. Whether or not he knew of this, Chris never found out because, unfortunately, he was killed in about 1935 in the Isle of Man.

Another famous rider was Ben Bickell, renowned for his copper-plated Chater Lea which he rode at Brooklands. Chris also remembers a Francis-Barnett with an incredibly noisy exhaust.

Bikes on the road at that time included Coulson Bs and 250 Round Tank BSAs. Down the road from Chris's home was a Miss Saunders who rode to work on a 250cc Levis two-stroke. He also remembers a Rover motorcycle. Near Chris's home was a motorcycle dealer who sold Rudges, and also in stock were the famous 'Four-Four' models which were four valve and four speed. They also had interconnected brakes. The front brake was a flat shoe operating on a flat, circular rim, not the usual V-shaped dummy belt rim.

In 1926 Chris's father bought him a bicycle, so Chris instantly took off the mudguards and put the front one on the back, converting it into a home-made dirt-track model. He and his friends used to broadslide vigorously on the gravel streets, blipping their imaginary throttles and generally behaving as kids do.

Further down the road lived Bill Holland, who rode a 350cc ohv BSA. He was a member of the Watford Club and used to race on the grass. Whenever he went to a meeting his mother would have a fit of the vapours, swooning and carrying on as she was sure that Billy would be killed. Until Billy finally arrived home from a meeting all the neighbours would stay with her, but instead of being a calming influence they merely added to the weeping, wailing and gnashing of teeth. When Billy finally returned and, to everyone's amazement, still alive, the visit to the undertaker had to be postponed yet again!

In 1927–28 Billy bought an overhead camshaft Chater Lea, which he sent to the factory and had tuned for alcohol fuel, also known as 'dope', with a high-compression piston and racing cams. One evening Chris heard the tremendous roar of an unsilenced motorcycle exhaust as a machine hurtled

A 1914 500cc Rudge Multi. The two most famous names in the variable-size engine-pulley system to enable a small variation in gear ratios were the Rudge Multi and the Zenith Gradua.

The famous Rudge Four-Four of 1926, now with a four-speed gearbox and a four-valve cylinder head.

down the main road. Rushing out to see it, he saw that it was Billy on his Chater Lea which he had just filled up at the Pratts garage around the corner. The fuel was probably PMS2 or RD1, the only dope then available.

The great day arrived when Billy raced his highly tuned Chater Lea. All the local children turned up to jeer at him as he still had his well-worn road tyres and was sliding all over the place. He could not afford new tyres as he had spent all his money on tuning the machine. Having fitted new tyres, however, he rode at Barnett, and for some reason his mother decided that rather than suffer at home she would go and see him killed! To everyone's amazement Billy wiped the board, and his mother became a dedicated fan. Bill Holland became a member of the Wembley speedway team in the 1930s and George Wilkes was the captain. Bill was a dedicated Rudge rider right to the end of his life.

In 1928 there was a motorcycle-football match between Watford and an Austrian club. The Austrian club riders all rode identical Puchs and wore identical jerseys, all new to Chris. The locals, however, rode a motley selection of bikes and all kinds of clothing. No matching jerseys for them! The match was held on the local football ground and did the turf no good at all, tearing it up badly. It would be totally out of the question today.

Ben Bickell on his 500cc Bickell/JAP at Brooklands in August 1931.

Doug Pirie, nearest the camera, rides his 500cc Excelsior/JAP at Brooklands in July 1932.

A 1928 Speedway Douglas which started the Speedway craze.

A 1930 Speedway Rudge which ousted the Douglas.

A 1931 Speedway JAP which beat the lot, though still with the Rudge frame.

An overhead camshaft AJS. Manufacturing a traditional overhead camshaft motorcycle engine with a vertical shaft and bevel gears, as in Velocettes and Nortons, was expensive so a chain-driven overhead camshaft was far cheaper. The chain drive on the AJS made for a rather ugly engine but worked well enough. The machine illustrated was restored by Mr Velocette himself, Ivan Rhodes, who always loved the 1920s Ajays.

The 1927 500cc BSA sloper. A successful design that gave excellent service.

The 1925 overhead camshaft Chater Lea at Brooklands. The vertical camshaft drive was topped by a horizontal disc, which was grooved to accept the inlet and exhaust rockers. Novel, indeed, but was it worth all the trouble?

The 1931 four-cylinder, spring frame, Matchless Silver Hawk. It was a very advanced design, but it never challenged the supremacy of the Ariel Square Four.

The family house at Bondgate, Castle Donington, today. The door on the right led to Chris's garage/workshop but is now incorporated into the house.

Speedway started in Australia, where the Douglas was supreme, and reached England in 1928, and because of Chris's father's job on the railway he was able to get to Wembley for a few pence to watch the racing. By then the Speedway Rudges were taking over, though some Speedway Douglases were still out there attempting to challenge the Rudge supremacy, and there were also a few Americans on their Harley Peashooters. There was no gearbox or brakes for any of the specialised speedway machines.

In 1925, Chris's sister was engaged to a motorcyclist who rode a Calthorpe, but sadly he was killed in a road accident. It was a great tragedy for Chris's sister.

When one of Chris's friends turned 16 he was at last able to realise his ambition to get on the road with his own motorcycle. He bought a side-valve Coventry Eagle, which he rode until he hit a car and ended up with a limp. That finished his friend's motorcycle days!

Chapter 4

THE FAMILY MOVES
TO DERBY

In 1930 Chris's father was posted to Derby, which was hit by severe flooding that year. Chris and one of his new friends, a fellow cyclist, thoroughly enjoyed riding through the flooded roads. During one tour of the town they came to Leaper Street and looked into a factory where the workers were doing their utmost to dry it out. His pal told Chris that this was where McEvoy motorcycles were made. McEvoy was an ex-Rolls-Royce privileged apprentice, an old Etonian who was financed by Sir Henry Birkin's brother. Sir Henry Birkin was the famous racing car driver, and his brother Archie rode in the Isle of Man where, unfortunately, he was killed. Their finances dried up and McEvoy's folded, but not, however, without making their mark in the world of motorcycles, making a range of big twins using Anzani or JAP engines. They also made an ultra-low speedway model with the engine mounted horizontally, though it is doubtful if any were ever actually sold.

One day Chris and his friend rode out of Derby on the London Road and finally arrived at Castle Donington village. They rode along Park Lane and came to the gates of Donington Hall which led to Donington Park. It was planned that racing would start there in 1932 and Chris, of course, decided he would go to see those races.

In 1930 one of his neighbours had a regular visitor who rode a mid-1920s Model 18 Norton. His name was Harry Skevington, and he later became friends with Chris. He also remembered seeing a big port AJS ridden very hard. The rider, he was to discover later, was the great Dusty Dunn.

The 1927 1,000cc McEvoy, raced at Brooklands by the great George Patchett and once owned by the author. Local enthusiast Stan Burnett fitted a two-of-everything pair of JAP alcohol speedway barrels on a common crankcase to produce an astonishing 78bhp. And the original racing JAP engine? Sold off by Stan for a fiver, if he was lucky!

In 1931 Chris bought a 1924 side-valve 250cc Raleigh for £2 10s. Chris was very proud of his machine, thinking it was a real racer because it could achieve 40mph downhill with a tail wind! One day, with his pal on the pillion, at Coxbench near Derby, they dashed across a level crossing when the Raleigh leapt up and down, throwing off its very slack magneto chain, jamming the chain and sprockets and bringing the bike to a halt. Chris's toolkit consisted of a screwdriver and a pair of pliers, so off came the magneto chain cover. He knew that the spark came about top dead centre on the compression stroke, so he put the chain back on and reset the ignition timing to something like that. Unfortunately the bike still would not start. He next took the magneto and timing covers off, and though he knew nothing about valve timing he did know that when the piston went down it sucked in the mixture and then came up on compression, but just when the valves opened and closed he had no idea.

There was a single camshaft on which were the exhaust and inlet cams, together with their tappets. He set the inlet camshaft to suck, the exhaust camshaft to blow, the ignition timing to about top dead centre on the compression stroke and tried again. This time the engine started, so he was an instant motorcycle mechanic!

That year Chris applied for an apprenticeship at Rolls-Royce, but when his headmaster heard of this he called in Chris's parents. He explained that as Chris had topped the matriculation results in mathematics, physics and chemistry with distinctions in physics, the first ever to do so under master 'Prism' Hastings, the physics master, he should remain at school for another two years.

Chris enjoyed riding his Raleigh around Derby, and on one occasion with his chum on the pillion a large dog ran into them, stopping the bike. Chris and his chum fell off, dusted themselves down, started the bike up again and carried on. In any case, they were used to falling off pushbikes. The dog raced away, apparently unhurt, so all was well. His longest ride with his pal on the pillion was to visit relatives in Huddersfield. They made it there and back in a day, which was no mean achievement.

One day in 1932 in Derby, Chris saw a racing Norton go hurtling by. In those days racing motorcycles were so different from road bikes that they were unmistakable. He wondered who the rider was and later found that it was Joe Hoult, who rode it that year in the Manx Grand Prix on the Isle of Man.

A 1923 350cc side-valve Raleigh similar to Chris's 1924 250cc model.

A 1924 350cc AJS.

Joe lived at Melbourne, a village about eight miles south of Derby, and Joe and Chris would eventually become great friends. In 1935 he bought that 1930 ex-works racing Norton from Joe and later raced it at Donington.

By the time Chris had seen Joe's Norton go racing past him, he decided that he needed something a bit faster than the Raleigh, so he went to a local dealer who had a 1926 350cc ohv AJS for sale. He bought it for £7 10s, which he had saved from his 2s 6d weekly pocket money plus the proceeds of the sale of the Raleigh to a friend. Chris wheeled the bike out of the shop and kickstarted it. The engine fired immediately. He got on this bike of monstrous power, put it into gear and released the clutch to cross the cobbles and tramlines. Halfway across, however, the engine continued to run but not drive! Chris pushed it back to the shop. The dealer quickly took the clutch to pieces revealing a broken clutch backplate which jammed the clutch into an open position. A new backplate was quickly fitted and, with the clutch apparently mended, off Chris went.

One morning, returning home on his AJS, Chris turned off the Ashbourne Road into a side street, where a car coming towards him swerved and hit him. His arm was caught on the door handle. Chris managed to stay on the bike and ride to the gutter with his right arm dangling, pulling up with his face almost touching the handlebars. He had to stall the engine as there was no way could he move the gear change lever, and he just stayed there in a daze. He was opposite Samways motorcycle business in Nuns Street, Derby, where the staff, seeing that Chris was obviously injured, took him in and gave him a cup of tea. When he felt a bit better Mr Samways put him on the pillion of his flat tank 500cc ohv Norton and took him home, at which point his mother took him straight to the doctor. The doctor decided that the arm was not broken, but Chris still has a crease in his right bicep which looks peculiar but does not bother him, and in a few weeks he was back riding again. Chris next found that the cast section of the frame where the gearbox was mounted had broken; however, he knew that a man who worked opposite Derby School named Dusty Dunn would weld it up for him. He took the engine and gearbox out of the frame, and then, riding his push bike with one hand and with the other hand on the handlebars of the AJS, he wobbled along to Dusty's place.

Dusty was the man that Chris had seen riding hard on his Big Port AJS. He was an unusual character with a very scarred face and a pronounced twitch. Both his head and his arms jerked frequently. He had some marvellous bikes in his charge, and Chris was delighted to look them over. Dusty worked for his father, who was a master plumber, and they used an old stable at the premises as their workshop. They had a gas fire in the workshop, and during the chilly English winters there was never a shortage of riders dropping in for warmth and a chat, as well as genuine paying customers. Dusty had ridden at Nottingham Speedway and had made a speedway special with a 500cc JAP engine lying horizontally in the frame. He still had one of the old spiked motorcycle tyres which had flat-headed coach bolts passing through the tread, with washers and nuts on the outside, but leaving about 2in of the bolt protruding. There was one every 2 or 3in with several across the tread, but in the 1920s the ACU banned them because of the injuries they could inflict if they hit a fallen rider, so these tyres were already part of motorcycle history, even then.

Dusty welded up the frame for a shilling or so, and Chris quickly rebuilt the bike but then had trouble with the carburettor. When riding flat out, his throttle would sometimes stick open with potentially disastrous results. Chris bought an Amac carburettor for a couple of bob from Dusty, and he later sold the original B&B to an enthusiast named Jim White, who put it on his AJS.

Among Dusty's motorcycles was a Speedway Douglas with a nickel-plated frame which had belonged to the great speedway rider Vic Huxley. Chris went to a race meeting with Dusty, where he raced the Douglas, but the flywheel came adrift. Dusty, however, assembled it with some corrosive chemical which appeared to hold it in place. By coincidence the rider who later bought the Douglas was to help Chris with spares for another machine. There was also an excellent overhead camshaft AJS with highly polished ports, connecting rod and flywheel. Dusty put this on the road, borrowing Chris's 350cc AJS number plates (MS6272).

One summer evening they rode the AJS up the road to check it. The bike was running on Castrol R and smoked heavily, which they hoped would settle

Barry and his big 'blown' Brough at Brooklands. E.C.E. Baragwanath and his Broughs were an indispensable part of the Brooklands scene for many years. Here he is at Brooklands in 1933.

35

down as the engine warmed up but, unfortunately, it failed to do so. They turned for home and checked the bike over to find that one of the return oil pipes that should have sucked oil from the crankcase was cracked, and it was sucking air rather than oil. Nevertheless, many years later that bike was still in use in Derby.

Dusty bought a 680cc ohv V-twin Brough Superior & sidecar for £27.10. It was absolutely pristine, but when Chris and Dusty went to collect it there were a few rain spots on it, for which the owner apologised profusely. Dusty sold the sidecar and replaced it with a racing chassis. The bike never went under cover again, and it was lucky to have an occasional tarpaulin thrown over it!

In late October and November 1932 the two young men amused themselves by riding around Derby and throwing bangers into cinema queues etc. The next day the local club had a run to a Derbyshire mine. It was the only club run that the two of them ever attended and, of course, sidecar passenger Chris had to lean all over the place and clamber over the outfit on every bend in the road. At the mine head they insisted that everyone remove any matches or similar from their pockets, but as Chris never carried matches he took no notice. Shortly after coming back to the surface, however, he realised he still had the matches from the previous night's foolish banger throwing! He kicked

A 680cc Brough Superior similar to the one owned by Dusty.

himself for such a silly mistake. On the way home the club stopped and Chris had to have a crack at riding the Brough, cavorting around with the sidecar wheel in the air, but at the next club meeting Dusty was ordered not to take his unruly passenger on future club runs.

When Chris first went to Dusty's he would just stand around and watch, but after a while he was allowed to clean things, and this graduated into him being allowed to tackle minor jobs and eventually to working alongside Dusty.

One day after school, having finished his homework, Chris put on his working clothes and arrived at Dusty's. There were four motorcyclists in their riding coats and waders, examining a spark plug which they passed around in their gloved hands, making comments about what was wrong with it. One would say 'The mixture is too weak'. 'No,' said another, 'the ignition timing is too far retarded'. Then, 'the centre electrode is faulty,' and so it went on.

Apparently just noticing the newly arrived Chris, they turned to him and asked what he thought? Chris was flattered that these experienced motorcyclists were asking him for his opinion, so he quickly held out his tender schoolboy hand and took the plug. He then screamed and dropped it. They had known he was coming, heated the plug and passed it quickly from one leather gloved hand to another, not holding it long enough to feel the heat, but it nearly burnt a hole through Chris's hand!

One night Dusty and Chris were busy working when one of the early Donington riders drove up in his car. He apparently had a date with one of the staff members from the hospital and was keen to take her out, but it was no deal unless he found a partner for her friend.

Would Dusty oblige? No. He then asked Chris and, a bit dubiously, he agreed. They drove to an up-market hostelry where the damsels joined them and then off to the country where the car was stopped and Chris was asked if he would like to take one of the girls for a walk. Chris was somewhat embarrassed because he was still in his working clothes, despite having apologised for that, but although his partner was several years older she was a very pleasant person and they wandered around chattering happily away. The other couple went in the opposite direction for a more romantic assignment!

Chapter 5

WORKING WITH DUSTY

Dusty was a keen radio ham and, on occasion, Chris would visit him when he was busy with his soldering iron making new connections. Chris noticed that he would touch various terminals with his finger and then do a bit more soldering, so after he had done this a few times Chris enquired as to what he was doing. Dusty explained that he was checking the voltage, finding whether it was high or low. Chris, of course, asked how he could tell and Dusty said it was by the feel, so Chris then had a try. He put his finger on six volts but felt nothing so then he tried a high-voltage terminal and just about got thrown on his back! Of course, Dusty, as a plumber, had very calloused hands and fingers and so when quickly touching 240 volts he could only feel a tingle, whereas Chris's softer schoolboy fingers really got a belt.

Dusty was a born engineer and could put his hand to anything. Chris once watched him lining up a pair of flywheels using a pair of 6in nails through two pieces of timber which in turn were nailed onto a longer piece of timber providing the base. The flywheels could then be rotated using the points of the nails as centres. He then visually lined up the alignment using a steel rule across the circumference of the flywheels as a guide.

Dusty and Chris decided to build a red-hot Norton for racing, so much work was put into polishing the flywheels, connecting rod, crankcase and head. The cams were modified, too. Crankcase in frame, Chris arrived one evening to find Dusty roaring with laughter. On enquiring what was so funny he was told that they had used a 16H side-valve Norton connecting rod which, at 8in, was an inch longer than the OHV rod, but rather than waste the work they had already completed they decided to make a hot-stuff side-valve engine instead! They found a Binks Mousetrap carburettor and, boy, how that side-valver could go. But where would you find a Mousetrap carburettor today? With little traffic on the roads in those days, Dusty and Chris raced around regardless.

One day they came across Michael McEvoy with his sidecar outfit parked at the roadside with his girlfriend Mona Simpson, later to become Michael's wife. Mona was the sister of racing man Jimmy Simpson, who was the first man to have ridden round the TT circuit at 60, 70 and 80mph. The bikes of those days, however, often failed to stand up to Jimmy's hard riding, and he failed to finish, giving Jimmy the title of 'Hard luck Simpson'. Dusty, of course, knew Michael McEvoy well and they chatted away – though shy schoolboy Chris did not utter a word!

In 1932, an old Etonian, over 6ft tall and powerfully built, arrived as a premium apprentice at Rolls-Royce. His father had paid Rolls-Royce £250 for the privilege of having his son paid 10 bob a week by the firm. His name was Michael Erskine, and he had two Speedway Rudges, which he raced locally. In those days he raced on minor grass-tracks as 'Smudger Smith', but he later became famous in the motorcycling world by manufacturing his Erskine StarRide speedway bikes. Frank Malouf from Sydney, an ex-speedway rider who captained the Long Eaton speedway team before Chris left England, knew Mike who managed one of Frank's speedway teams.

One night, although Chris explained that he was broke, Mike insisted that he accompany him and some speedway pals on a pub crawl. Chris had to owe him for the shandies he drank!

At about this time a man advertised in one of the motorcycling periodicals that he wanted to come to Derby to race at Donington Park, and Dusty replied to the advert. He was an Indian named Rio Mirza who worked for De Havilland. He brought his racing Norton to Derby on the

McEvoy factory. Michael McEvoy only manufactured motorcycles in Derby between 1926 and 1929, but he was a talented engineer who produced a twin-tube 'Duplex' frame and designed a 350cc three-valve overhead camshaft engine, not unlike a Velocette. It was semi-unit construction with the gearbox bolted to the engine. His masterpiece was the four-cylinder in-line overhead camshaft engine, but it only existed as a mock-up, and none were produced. It is in the forefront of the photograph, and the ohc single is on the right.

Behind the four is a speedway machine with a horizontally mounted engine and this, I feel, means that the photograph is of the 1928 Olympia Motorcycle Show, as speedway did not arrive in England until 1928. The machine behind that is a Villiers engined 250cc two stroke. The machine on the far right at the back is not clear enough to identify. The 350cc ohc engine/gearbox unit is on a plinth in the middle of the stand.

sidecar chassis of another Norton, and Chris's mother put him up for a couple of nights. Chris went to Donington as his racing mechanic. It was a very wet day, and it appeared that he took none too kindly either to the wet conditions or the speed of the other riders in practice, so he did not race. Some years later he joined Rolls-Royce in Derby and helped Chris up the career ladder. He later moved to Australia, and they kept in touch until Mirza's death.

Another remarkable enthusiast that Chris knew was Frank Platt from Belper, whose parents had moved around the country so often that Frank did not have much of an education. When Chris got in contact with him again some years later, it was his wife who wrote in return. Frank was an absolute genius at tuning motorcycles and making everything in his well-equipped machine shop, which was so packed with machinery and flying belts that a friend said 'Put a foot wrong and you're marmalade'. He was, of course, a rider but not a racing man, so he got another rider to ride a Velocette that he tuned at Donington in 1933. If Chris had not been thought of as so wild then Frank could have considered letting him ride the Velocette but Frank was, no doubt, aware that Chris was as likely to break it as not.

There were a number of motorcyclists riding around Derby that neither Chris nor Dusty ever got to know. One rode a Grindlay Peerless and always looked as if he was going to a wedding. A double for Rudolph Valentino, his hair was always slickly plastered down and he always wore a blue coat. Why he rode a bike at all they never could tell. Another was the local bookmaker who drove from pub to pub picking up his two bob each way from the punters, riding his four-cylinder Silver Hawk Matchless. He later rode a 350cc International Norton which he rarely got out of second gear. As he never ventured out of the built-up area, Chris and his pals would watch him ride by thinking what a tremendous waste it was.

In 1933 Chris heard of a flat-tank 500cc Model Eighteen Norton that was for sale. It was owned by a man who lived about seven miles from Chris's home who was willing to swap it for his AJS. As the AJS was not

An 498cc AJS with twin-port ohv engine and instrument panel mounted on the tank top.

Elegance and quality: the 493cc twin-port Sunbeam.

A stylish 350cc side-valve Douglas twin. Old friend and Scott fanatic Maurice Patey so admired these 1931 Douggies that he beautifully restored a 1931 600.

taxed Chris and his pal borrowed his mother's clothes line for a tow rope and they alternately rode Chris's bicycle towing the AJS. On their arrival Chris fired up the Norton to ride it home and his pal rode the bicycle.

The year 1931 was a memorable one for motorcycle design and pointed the way in which design and style would take for almost half a century. Twin ports were all the rage at the time, though this was a styling trend that would not continue. Here are some examples:

Chris had not owned the Model Eighteen Norton long when he decided to take the engine apart, and he was amazed to find the remains of a cast-iron piston in the crankcase. The flywheels were quite well polished, as apparently the broken pieces of piston had acted as laps and polished them up. He later found that the previous owner had experienced a failed cast-iron piston, fitted an aluminium replacement at the roadside and then sold it on. The new owner found the scrap iron in the crankcase and decided to pass the bike on to Chris, not realising that the bits had merely done a good job in polishing up the flywheels.

Dusty Dunn's father employed a man who had bought two identical Rudges. One had front-end damage and the other had been on fire, so he

Two more elegant designs from 1931. Top-left: 500cc Norton. Top-right: KTP 350cc Velocette with coil ignition. Both machines had the fashionable twin ports.

A 1919 400cc ABC. An outstanding machine for its day: front and rear suspension, unit construction with four-speed gate change like a car, horizontally opposed ohv engine set across the frame and dynamo lighting when everyone else had acetylene lighting. Surely the inspiration for the first BMW introduced in 1923, though they said that they had never heard of it! The BMW was side-valve, not ohv, no rear suspension but, of course, shaft drive like every other BMW since.

made one good bike out of the bits. Delighted with his handiwork, he rode the bike to and from London for a weekend, but not until he got back home did he realise that he had the front number plate off one of the bikes and the other number plate on the rear.

At about this time a rider named Alf Hall, who was in the insurance business, took his bike, a 1928 250 Ariel Colt, to Dusty for repair. Alf asked Chris to ride with him on the pillion around his rural 'parish' to visit his customers. It seemed like a great idea to Chris because, as he was on two shillings and sixpence a week pocket money and petrol about a shilling per gallon, with a pint of oil a similar price, it did not leave much left, so without paying these costs Chris got a free ride and felt he was on to a winner!

Back on the road, another free ride came when one of Dusty's customers had his sloper BSA break down at Skegness, about 100 miles away. Chris took him on his pillion to 'Skeggy', hitched a tow rope onto the Beezer and proceeded home. On arrival the owner swore he had been screaming at Chris all the way back to slow down and also claimed that the BSA had never travelled so fast!

After the motorcycle business folded, Michael McEvoy continued in the same Leaper Street, Derby, works concentrating on supercharging. He was the British agent for Zoller superchargers. Here are two examples: An MG and his own Austin saloon which, believe it or not, he used competitively. He also fitted a supercharger to a 1934–35 Val Page-designed Triumph vertical twin (not to be confused with the late 1930s Edward Turner-designed twins) as a mobile test bed.

Chris used to make a speciality of departing from Dusty's garage which was about 50 yards down a side street. Dusty would go up to the main road, which in those days had very little traffic, and signal to Chris when the road was all clear. Chris would ride the Norton with the throttle wide open, and when he reached the corner he would power slide left onto the main road which had cobbles and tram tracks. Chris shudders when he thinks back on it now.

Dusty taught Chris to solder, braze and weld, though he never offered him the opportunity to do work at which he was extremely talented. He would make stained-glass windows by burning the lead in between the pieces of glass, which was highly skilled work.

While he always had a dram of whisky when they were racing, Dusty was not really a boozer. He regularly worked to 9pm at night before going across the road to the local pub, though he would never encourage Chris to go. Chris would stay behind in the workshop and get on with some more work. Foolishly, Chris was under the impression that cider was just apple juice and not alcoholic. When out in the sidecar with Dusty he would have a couple of beers and Chris would have a cider or two, feeling wobbly under the influence every now and again! Chris well remembers him protesting on one occasion when some fellow riders were telling Chris to 'Be a man and drink some beer.'

On occasion, Dusty would take along a solo motorcycle to race meetings and would race both sidecar and solo. After the racing Chris would have a ride, and he always looked upon this as a bit of fun rather than a serious attempt at this kind of racing, as his ambition was to race on the road. He looked forward to having a competitive bike and having a go at Donington. At one meeting he saw, of all things, a 1920 400cc ABC competing. At another meeting he was allowed to have a ride on a Speedway BSA.

Chapter 6

CHRIS AND DUSTY'S GRUDGE MATCH

One of the most memorable of Chris and Dusty's sidecar races was when they went to a non-ACU racetrack. Of course they did not race as 'Dusty and Chris's but as champions of wherever, and they were matched against a rider named Hoff who was also supposed to be some kind of champion. He was also a philanthropist and the match was some sort of charity function organised by him. It was billed as the big grudge race. Hoff was a Leicester dealer and had a 600cc Douglas outfit with a barely 2ft-wide chassis, so it was very manoeuvrable and handled almost like a solo.

Dusty, according to the layout of the track, would adjust the sidecar attachments to lay the bike over to left or right dependent upon the number and nature of the bends. This attention to detail, together with help from Johnny Walker, was one of the reasons why they could get round at such a speed.

In the sidecar race Dusty and Chris were competing directly against Hoff, and not only was it a big grudge event, but it was also announced on the PA system that the competing riders had to be physically prevented from actually fighting. Dusty and Chris won the first race, but in the second race they allowed Hoff to get ahead while they pretended to be making every attempt to pass him. Dusty was swerving and pumping the throttle while Chris climbed all over the outfit like a demented monkey. It was an exciting finish with Hoff just ahead. The third race was to be the decider.

After several solo events the grand final was announced. They had been prevented from having a punch-up so who would win? Chris and Dusty knew

C.W.G. 'Bill' Lacey on his 500cc Grindlay Peerless/JAP covered over 103 miles in one hour at Brooklands on 1 August 1928, becoming the first man to cover over 100 miles in an hour on a British track. His beautifully prepared machines gave him the title 'Nickel Plate Lacey'.

A 1924 500cc four-valve Triumph Ricardo, designed by the great engineer Harry Ricardo, who also designed engines for World War One tanks. The firm is still going strong today. These machines sold well and continued in use for many years.

A 1929 400cc narrow-angle (26 degrees) spring frame side-valve Matchless Silver Arrow. The cylinders were in-line and cast in one block, with cooling fins common to both barrels. My old friend, Harry Tunaley, had one.

A design well ahead of its time, the 1928 500cc Ascot Pullin, with unit construction engine/gearbox and hydraulic brakes. You would have thought that it would have sold like hot cakes but, although motorcyclists of the 1920s and 1930s clamoured for new designs, when it came to actually handing over their hard-earned brass – and it was hard earned in those days – they bought conventional machines instead. Few were sold, and Chris only ever saw one.

The Land's End Trial was a famous annual event in the motorcycle calendar for many years and included the famous Porlock Hill. The machine given a push by a friendly policeman in this 1925 event is a two-speed Scott. The riding gear is typical of the times: leather helmet, goggles, riding breeches, long stockings and brogues, topped off with a riding coat.

they were going to win, and they confidently lined up on the start line. Whether it was because Dusty had consumed too many whiskies or because Hoff was really on the ball, they were surprised to find themselves second into the first corner. Naturally, they intended to pass at the first opportunity, but, try as they might, by the fourth lap they were still second. The final corner was a sweeping left-hander with the finish right at the end of the bend, so you did not have time to straighten up before you crossed the line. They went into this right on Hoff's tail. Dusty kept winding the throttle and Chris was hanging over the sidecar wheel but, even so, it still kept rising. Just before the finish line they passed Hoff on the outside, but the outfit decided that it had had enough as they crossed the finish line and Dusty, the outfit and Christopher all became projectiles. Nevertheless, they were still judged the winners. The spectators certainly got their money's worth!

Chapter 7

CHRIS LOSES HIS LICENCE

O
ne evening a couple of riders called in at Dusty's while Chris was working there. One was Joe Hoult from Melbourne on the 1930 Ulster Grand Prix-winning Norton which he had raced in the 1932 Isle of Man Grand Prix, and the other was Bob Vesey, a fantastic Donington rider on his 1924 Frank Platt-tuned Model 18. This Norton had a three-speed close-ratio gearbox, where bottom was in the middle. As there were no positive stop gear changes in those days this was a great help as bottom to second was hard down, second to top hard up and top to second hard down, so the only gear you had to 'feel' was second to bottom. At first it seemed funny to have bottom in the middle, but when you consider the advantages when adapted to foot change it was a great idea. Of course, the Sturmey Archer gearbox was originally hand change. At that time Chris had no idea that he would later own both those Nortons.

Bob said that they were going up the Duffield road for what they called 'A bit of a dust', so Chris asked if he could come along and followed them for six or seven miles up the road. When Chris saw them turn round at the far end of a straight he also turned round and was, of course, in the lead. Coming to a bend with the throttle wide open, Chris thought he would show these fellows a thing or two, but halfway round there was an explosion of sound in his right ear, and Bob Vesey just ripped past him, followed by Joe Hoult. Chris realised that he was not as good a rider as Joe and Bob and had not been travelling all that fast after all, but he was overjoyed when Dusty later told him that Bob had said: 'That kid can ride.'

Bob on his 1924 Norton regularly used to beat riders on more modern machines including International Nortons. He also beat Doug Pirie on an Excelsior with the Speedway JAP engine, as well as Crasher White, Jock Muir and a few other Manx Grand Prix riders.

Chris asked Bob Vesey for a few clues on to how to improve his riding at Donington and ensure the best performance. Bob replied that on a fast bike any fool could go down the straight as fast as the other fellow but on a slow machine you could make up a lot of what you might have lost on the straight by late braking into the bends. Chris took this to heart and later practised it at Donington. Sadly, Bob was killed in practice at Donington in August 1933 riding a borrowed Velocette. This was a dreadful blow to his family, Chris, Dusty and Bob's other friends.

A few weeks later Chris was riding near Derby when he was passed by an old schoolmate whose father had bought him a Bullnose Morris. How could a Bullnose have gone that fast? With him were a chum and a couple of girls, so Chris had to demonstrate how fast he could go. He went round a bend very fast, hit a pothole and put the bike into a tank slapper. Fortunately he managed to hang on, regain control and carry on. After a couple of miles he decided to

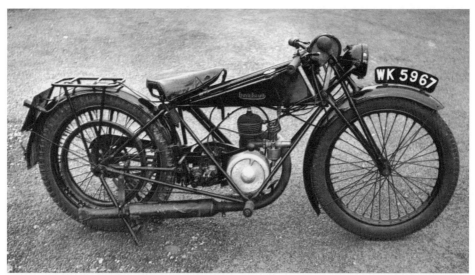

A late 1920s 150cc Villiers engined Francis Barnett. Bread and butter motorcycling! The frame consisted of a number of straight tubes bolted together.

A 1930 Excelsior with 500cc JAP engine. A typical big thumper of the era.

turn back and have a look at this dangerous pothole, but when he got there the village policeman, seeing his distinctive fire-engine red tank, flagged him down and the result was a summons. So Chris had to appear in court accused of dangerous driving. The magistrate was the formidable Brigadier General Meynell, a real hunting, fishing and shooting fire-eater who considered motorcycles to be an abomination as they frightened the horses.

Having heard the evidence, Brigadier General Meynell announced that Chris was a road hog, fined him five pounds and in September 1933 cancelled his licence for 12 months. Chris was very upset indeed about this. He did not have the five pounds anyway, though that was not too bad, but the loss of his licence was a tragedy. Much to his surprise, there was a shuffling in the court and his father came forward to pay the fine. That evening the local paper carried the headline 'Magistrate calls Derby schoolboy a road hog'.

After he lost his licence he would accept any opportunity to ride pillion. One of Dusty's regular visitors had an almost-new 500cc Cotton/JAP, and when he offered Chris a ride on the pillion to Whatstandwell Bridge Chris jumped at the chance. At the bridge there are two 90-degree bends over the River Derwent. The lads used to congregate there to watch the traffic and other motorcyclists take the bends.

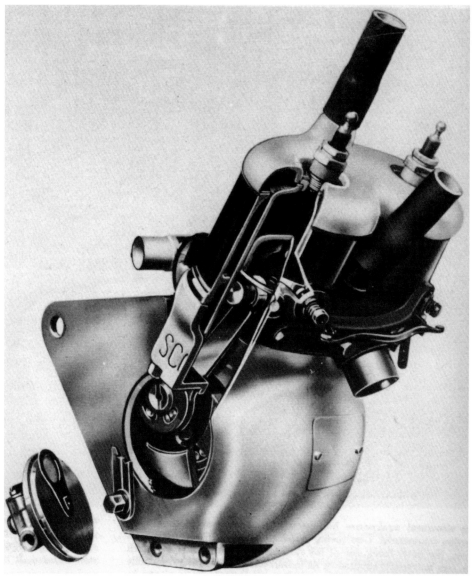

The Scott engine of 1925. Alfred Scott was a brilliant, innovative engineer, and the concept of his engines was far from the conventional. Tom Ward of Derby had worked with Scott and ran a one-man mail order business repairing Scott engines and gearboxes. He maintained that nothing compared with the Scott engine for function and simplicity. This engine is a 1925 Super Squirrel, showing the overhung crank assembly and drive for the Best and Lloyd oil pump. A surprise feature was that you could remove the circular crankcase doors and replace the big-end rollers in a matter of minutes.

Chris had no idea of this rider's ability, and as soon as they left the town he opened up on the first straight. There was a sharpish bend at the end of the straight. As they entered it Chris thought they were going too fast and would never get round it at that speed. Sure enough the rider had, indeed, entered the bend far too fast. Realising this all too late, the rider banked the bike hard over, desperately hit the brakes and down the road they went, bouncing along for many yards. After they had picked themselves up and dusted themselves off they got back on the Cotton, but the rider decided that enough was enough and, much to Chris's annoyance, off they went back to Derby where he dropped Chris off. He never saw him again!

Chapter 8

CHRIS GOES TO BLACKPOOL

nother pillion ride was with a man named Reg Webster, who had a dance band and asked Chris to ride pillion with him to Blackpool. He had fallen out with his wife, who had gone to live in Blackpool, so he wanted to see her and have a bit of company on the 200-mile run. It was a lovely day so off they went, and as they approached Blackpool a fellow Derby motorcyclist, who raced Ajays, drew level with them with his mate on the pillion.

They, too, were heading for Blackpool, so Reg said that he had some accommodation booked and that there would probably be vacancies available and invited the other riders along. When they arrived they found that the place was almost full, but they could put three of them up, four at a pinch. At that time Chris was 18 but only looked 15, so the lady of the house suggested that he could sleep in a big attic with all the females and a couple of kids. Chris said 'No' as he wanted to be with his mates, but when he saw some of the girls coming down from the attic next morning he wondered what sort of an idiot he was!

They slept with the window open but got bitten by some sort of bugs. Freddie Blomfield and his chum went off on the Ajay, Reg saw his wife, and eventually they set off back to Derby.

By then, English summer weather had set in, and they rode along in a steady drizzle. When they got to Wigan they hit a bend paved with wet, greasy cobblestones and down they went. Reg was very concerned that Chris was all right, but having been assured that he was all that mattered was 'Let's get going again!' Eventually they arrived at Derby, but it was nearly midnight. Chris was wet through and cold as he did not have proper riding gear, only bicycle leggings and a rain coat. The leggings had a strap and buckle under the instep, which tinkled as Chris walked home from the main road where Reg had dropped him.

Chris's father retired in 1934, and they moved to a house in Castle Donington with a large orchard. The house is opposite the Turks Head pub, and the orchard extended well along Park Lane. The orchard is now a housing estate, with 'Peartree this' and 'Orchard that' street names.

By then Chris had bought the Vesey Norton for £8. It really was a great performer but, of course, it had no lighting. So Chris fitted a small bicycle lamp and a tail lamp powered by flashlight batteries. The rear battery was held on by rubber bands, and you 'lit up' by tucking the bare wire end onto contact under the rubber. At the front he used a cycle lamp with a .08 watt bulb, which produced such a tiny glimmer that he had to put his hand in front of it to make sure it was on! Chris was working shifts as a staff member at the British Celanese laboratory in Derby, carrying out chemical checks in the plant that turned Acetic acid into Aldehyde, so he did plenty of night riding.

An early 1920s Dunelt two stroke. Dunelts had a two/diameter piston to increase crankcase compression.

A mid-1920s Cotton. In the 1920s the unusual Cotton triangulated frame handled better than many of its contemporaries. The great Stanley Woods won his first TT on one in 1923, the 350cc Junior. In my opinion they always looked better in their flat tank days and looked rather ungainly with the newer saddle tanks.

The bike had no toolbox, so he carried a pocket full of spanners and, thus equipped, he rode for nine months.

Chris's friend, Harry Skevington, bought a brand new 1932 Model 18 Norton, and he and Chris would go out riding together. He was a very fast and stylish rider, and Chris wished he could reach the same standard. One Sunday they were on the Matlock Road going round a series of bends. Chris was riding close to his back wheel thinking how well Skev was heeling his bike over and swinging round the bends, until he realised that he was doing exactly the same. As Chris was not even trying very hard his confidence increased from that time onwards. Skev gave Chris a 1932 Norton pin badge that he still treasures. One evening Chris and Skev decided to go out and check on the local talent at Ilkeston. It was a beautiful clear night, and following Skev up a steady rise at about 70mph Chris lost the primary chain. It was a fairly narrow country road with no kerb or guttering, just grass verges and ditches, but luckily it was a moonlit night and the chain was easily located lying on the road. A spare spring clip and a pair of pliers in Chris's Belstaff riding coat pocket and they were away again in a few minutes. Chris has not recorded what they made of the local talent!

Skev and Chris experienced a most interesting interlude in early 1935. Skev's father, separated from his mother, lived in Blackpool, and Skev had seen little of him. As Skev was about to get married he thought that it would be a good idea to take his bride-to-be to meet his dad, and Chris decided to go with them.

The weather was dreadful, and when they got to Warrington the Norton packed up with water in the magneto. Chris pushed it into a nearby garage and asked if he could stay in the shelter to repair it. He then dismantled the magneto, dried it out satisfactorily, re-fitted it and then awaited Skev's return and so back to Derby. Skev and his girlfriend eventually arrived at Blackpool and knocked on his father's door. His dad came to the door, and Skev said 'Hello'. Skev then said 'Don't you know me?', to which his dad replied: 'Well, I know your face'. 'I'm Harry', said Skev. The response was 'Harry, of course, what was it that you wanted, Harry?' After Harry announced that he was his son the penny dropped. Skev introduced his girlfriend and all went well. Eventually he arrived back at Warrington, and they all got on their way home.

Skev's Norton had no dynamo, only an accumulator, but a freshly charged battery would give a good light for some time, particularly as the bike had a very low wattage rear light. Chris tucked in behind him and kept the dim rear light in sight. Chris kept his peaked cap pulled well down over his eyes and a scarf across the lower part of his face as he went, blinking through the rain, over the seemingly endless miles of hills and dales between Warrington and Derbyshire. He had absolutely no idea of where they were, as his entire concentration was on keeping that rear light in sight. Very few of the places they went through had street lights, but at least Chris knew that they were heading for home.

Suddenly Chris realised that the rear light that he had been following so closely was now approaching him at high speed, so he swerved to avoid it, then realised that Skev was turning right.

Skev, fortunately, had looked over his shoulder as rear view mirrors were unheard of then. He realised what was happening and pulled part way into the corner, but Chris had to lay his bike well over to miss him, skidded right across the right angle corner, hit the kerb and was thrown into a shop doorway. The doorway had two pairs of large boots in it at Chris's eye level, and when he looked up there was a sergeant and a constable sheltering from the rain! They had arrived at Ashbourne where the Derby Road branches off to the right at a T-junction. Chris always remembered this whenever he saw this junction when going through Ashbourne. Come to think of it, so do I, as the junction remains unchanged.

The first thing the sergeant said to him was 'What were you doing trying to pass him on that corner?' To which Chris replied, none too diplomatically, 'Don't talk bloody daft, I've followed him all the way from Blackpool!' Not the most tactful reply. By then Skev had pulled up alongside and a few more questions were being asked. Chris was doing his best to talk himself further into trouble when the church clock struck midnight. Skev, just over a year older but years older in common sense, quickly said 'That's midnight and you are nearly out of petrol.' (Not true.) 'If we hurry we will get some at the garage down the road'. So Chris ran and bump started his Norton, leaped aboard and they were away. Had he been left alone the next thing would have been the policeman getting out his notebook.

One of the famous sidecar experts in the 1930s was Kim Collett, who managed a large motorcycle dealership in Oxford. For some reason he was looking for a new sidecar passenger, and Chris thought it would be great to race at Donington with such a rider. He rode down to Oxford to meet Kim, taking a workmate on the pillion. It was a rainy day and they arrived wet through, finding Kim enjoying a cup of tea. He asked if they would also like a cup, but silly Chris said 'No thank you'. They had a good chat, but in view of the 100 miles between their homes he thought it would be too difficult to form a regular partnership, so Chris never rode as a sidecar passenger with the great Kim Collett.

When they went outside to get on their machines ready for the return journey his pal, Tunnicliffe, wanted to kick Chris's backside as he would have so appreciated the hot cup of tea that Chris had foolishly turned down!

Chris had no lights on his Norton, but Tunnicliffe's bike had the benefit of dynamo lighting. They were riding down a road with red brick walls on either side, obviously the boundary of a large estate. Looking ahead, Chris saw a dark patch between the walls. Assuming that the road went into this, he headed for the gap. Tunnicliffe, however, swung to the left at about 40mph while Chris, taken by surprise, carried on up the driveway of some ancestral manor. Thank goodness the gates were open!

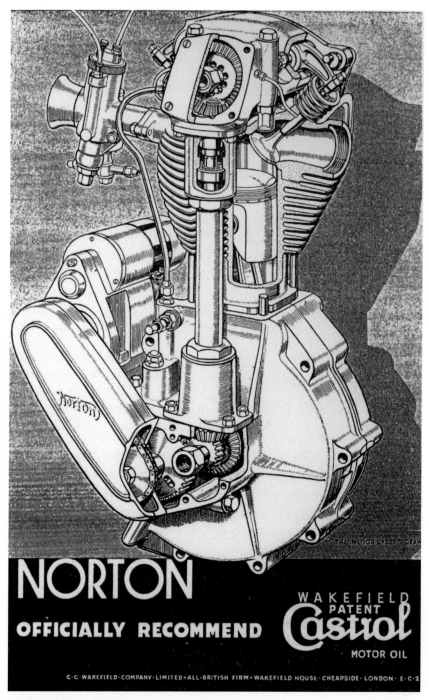

NORTON

OFFICIALLY RECOMMEND

WAKEFIELD
PATENT
Castrol
MOTOR OIL

C·C·WAKEFIELD·COMPANY·LIMITED·ALL·BRITISH·FIRM·WAKEFIELD HOUSE·CHEAPSIDE·LONDON·E·C·2

The Carroll-designed overhead camshaft Norton engine.

Chapter 9

THE OVERHEAD CAMSHAFT NORTON

T he first overhead valve Norton was introduced in 1922 and immediately proved its worth. The 1924 models swept the board with a dazzling display of wins. Alec Bennett became the frst man to win three major classics: the TT, The French GP and the Belgian GP, all on different examples of standard Model 18s – there were no special works models then. Immediately after the TT, Brooklands racer Bert Denly took the ohv Norton to Montlhery and raised the 500cc hour record to 100.57mph, the frst time that a 500 had beaten the 'ton' for an hour.

So how could Norton ever produce a better engine than that? They were going to show the world that they could.

In the winter of 1926–27 Walter Moore designed the first overhead camshaft Norton engine, a basic design that was destined to transform Norton's fortunes. It was not a very pretty design, but it certainly produced results. At the same time he designed a new cradle frame.

During TT practice, *Motorcycling* magazine had a speed trap at Sulby, where Stanley Woods and Joe Craig on their Nortons were fastest at 93.7mph. During the race Stanley Woods was well in the lead, leading Alec Bennett by four minutes on the fourth lap after a record lap at 70.99mph. Unfortunately, however, Stanley's clutch failed and Alec Bennett went on to win at 68.41mph ahead of Jimmy Guthrie on a New Hudson prepared by the legendary tuner Bert LeVack, with Tommy Simister on a Triumph third. It was a marvellous send-off for the new design.

Alec Bennett after his successful 1924 TT ride on the Model 18.

Jimmy Shaw on his way to riding his Model 18 to victory in the 100-mile sand race at Magilligan Strand, 1924.

Chris Harrison with his 1930 ex-works Norton, ridden to victory by Stanley Woods in the Ulster Grand Prix and raced by Chris at Donington, 1936–38.

The great Jimmy Guthrie after finishing in second place behind teammate Tim Hunt in the 1931 Senior TT. The new Caroll-designed engines had found their unbeatable form and went on to dominate the racing scene in the 1930s.

In late 1927 a road-going version of the overhead camshaft model was offered for the 1928 season at £95, together with the ES2 at £85. Both had the new cradle frames and, for the first time, saddle tanks. It was the first time that Norton had sold machines with anything other than flat tanks.

These 1928 over-the-counter models were capable of an astonishing 90mph. Tim Hunt bought one, rode it in the Scottish Six Days Trail and then in the Amateur TT (forerunner of the Manx Grand Prix). He not only won the race but also beat Stanley Woods's lap record at 71.05mph, the only rider ever to set the September lap record at a higher speed than the TT.

For the 1928 racers the cylinder head was re-designed, but it was not a success until they reverted to the 1927 design. In 1929 Walter Moore had left to join NSU, where he designed overhead camshaft engines for them, inspired by his design for Norton. The great Joe Craig decided that a new design was required and set to work with the head of the design office, Arthur Carroll, who had been Walter Moore's assistant. The result was the far neater Arthur Carroll design, though Joe Craig had made a major contribution. This was the basic design that would put Norton in the forefront of racing right through the 1930s and even into the post-war years. The very first example was rushed to the 1929 Show at Olympia. It had the new Carroll bottom half but still with the Walter Moore head, though we do not know whether it was a runner or not.

Like many new designs, the 1930 Carroll-designed engines required development to realise their potential, and they struggled to achieve success that year. In the TT the push-rod Rudges were unbeatable, but towards the end of the season Stanley Woods won the Ulster Grand Prix, then the French Grand Prix. This was the very machine that Chris was later to acquire.

The new road-going Carroll engines were offered at the 1931 Show for the 1932 season, and from 1931 onwards the racing Nortons started on their incredible run of successes, with Tim Hunt achieving the first-ever TT Senior/Junior double, i.e. 350 and 500.

Chapter 10

1931

– THE YEAR OF CHANGE

In 1931 there were several major changes in the motor and motorcycling world. It is not generally realised today that the 20mph speed limit was not repealed until 1931 – though no one had taken any notice of it for years! At the same time the motorcycle age limit was raised from 14 to 16, and insurance became compulsory for cars and motorcycles but was RTA (Road Traffic Act) only, which covered damage to persons but not property. So for a few years there were no speed limits until the 30mph limit was introduced for built-up areas.

Phil Heath was one of those larger-than-life characters in the world of motorcycling. A Leicestershire man who worked as a journalist, he was also an ex-Continental racing man and lifelong motorcycle enthusiast. He owned a 1931 500 ex-works racing Norton virtually identical to Chris's. Towards the end of his life he considered himself very hard up, and when someone needed a gearbox for an identical Norton Phil took the gearbox out of his machine and sold it to him – a great mistake.

One summer, Chris was staying with us. He was then in his 80s. His old friend Titch Allen, founder of the Vintage Motorcycle Club, got in touch. He knew the man who had bought Phil's Norton, less gearbox. His Christian name escapes me, but his father's name was Bill Lacey, i.e. identical to the great Brooklands rider/tuner, though he was no relation. Titch, by a miracle, had found a correct gearbox, and young Lacey had re-fitted it and made a beautiful job of completely restoring the machine. Titch had told the Laceys about Chris and arranged for them to bring the

Tim Hunt rides to victory on his Norton with its new Carroll-designed ohc engine in the 1931 Senior TT. It was the first-ever Senior/Junior double.

Norton over for Chris, not just to see, but to have a ride on and revive old memories. So, for the first time in over half a century, Chris was, once again, in the saddle of a racing Norton. How did he get on? Wonderfully well, riding it with style and complete confidence, though he confessed to me later that it had brought a lump to his throat. The Norton is now in the National Motorcycle Museum.

So what happened to Chris's 1930 ex-works 500? He sold it in 1939, but then came the war and so many young men went into the forces, leaving their motorcycles either in a garden shed or in the backyard with an old raincoat for protection. An enormous number of these men never returned, homes were bombed and families moved. As a result many of these now rusting old motorcycles, of no interest to anyone, were dumped for scrap. Chris's Norton has not survived, so it seems certain to have suffered the same fate.

A 1934 350cc KTT Velocette.

The great Billy Wing of Daybrook, who was the Nottingham Velocette agent, was a regular Donington rider. At one Donington meeting, Chris watched him come out of Hollywood, now swept away, and round the Craner Curves which, even today, are much as they were then. He was travelling at about 80mph along the right-hander and then banked hard into the left-hander and lost it. He and his bike went onto the thick, wet grass with Billy sliding, bumping and rolling down the slope until he slowed to about 10mph when sliding on his back. With his feet outstretched, his heels dug in and he shot to his feet with his crashed bike about 100 yards ahead of him, knocking over the post that held the start and finish banner.

Willing helpers raced forward to clear all the ropes, etc away before the next rider could hit them. Many years later Chris told this story to 'young' Titch Allan (Titch is a couple of months younger than Chris), and he told Chris that he, too, had seen this incident happen but had never before met anyone else who had.

In the January 1989 issue of *Classic Bike* there is a picture of Billy Wing racing at Donington and also a picture of two friends of Chris: one was Eric Lewis, from whom Chris bought his racing leathers in 1934, and the other was Roy Armitage, who rode a KTT Velocette at Donington. There is also a photograph of Freddie Craner, who organised everything that happened at Donington.

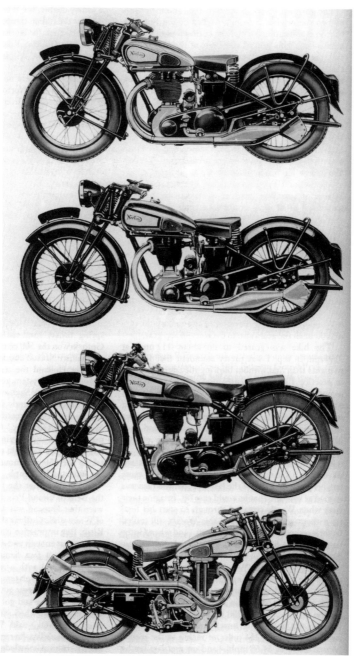

These are 1934 models: (Top) 500cc Model 20. Like the Model 18, but with twin ports. (Second) 350cc Model 55. Twin-port version of the pushrod Model 50. (Third) 350cc Model 40. The smaller of the two overhead-camshaft models. (Bottom) 350cc Model 55, again with upswept exhaust system.

Chapter 11

FREDDIE CRANER

– THE MAN WHO STARTED THE DONINGTON RACING CIRCUIT

Freddie Craner was an ex–TT rider. He lived at Coppice Lodge, Donington Park, and as Chris was a local boy when he started racing in the 1930s he would just ride over to hand in his entries and therefore got to know Fred and his wife quite well. He remembers that Freddie's wife was a very pleasant lady, very different from her husband who would smartly tell you to clear off if he was busy! They had no children. Chris has described him as stout and below average height – usually wearing plus-fours. A good head of hair and a ruddy complection completes the picture. 'He looked much like a farmer,' Chris once said.

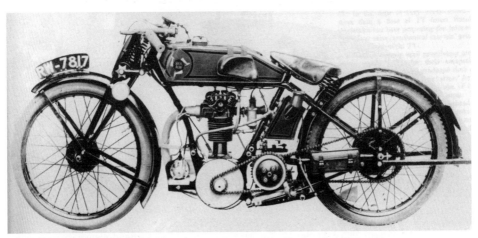

A late 1920s 250cc racing Rex Acme.

A 1929 500cc V-twin James.

Freddie was another of the great Derby characters who left his imprint on the world of motorcycling and motorsport. According to racing man Phil Heath, Freddie died suddenly after an operation in 1949, aged 49. But he worked at Rolls-Royce, Derby, before World War One and had his first motorcycle in 1913, so surely he must have been born about 1899.

I knew Freddie towards the end of his life when he had mellowed, and he was happy to reminisce about his motorcycling days. The saying 'Once a motorcyclist, always a motorcyclist' certainly applied to Freddie.

On the outbreak of war he joined the Royal Naval Air Service as a Petty Officer, working on Rolls-Royce armoured cars. He served in several theatres of war in Africa then back in the UK where he helped to install engines in the rigid airships R24, 25 and 27, built at Selby. While working on Rolls-Royce engines he was very interested in the servo clutch on the Rolls-Royce dynamos and decided to utilise the same system for motorcycle brakes.

During his service on armoured cars he met Cyril Pullin, winner of the 1914 TT and later designer of the Ascot Pullin. He inspired Freddie with tales of racing at the TT. Freddie also spent some time at Wormwood Scrubs: no, not as a prisoner, it was then an army depot!

After the war it was back to Rolls-Royce, this time as a car tester. In those days Rolls-Royce cars were sold as a chassis and the bodies were

A Donington meeting in the early 1930s. These are the famous Craner Curves.

commissioned from various specialised makers, including Barker, Park Ward, Vanden Plas and many others. Freddie would race round Derbyshire on the Rolls-Royce chassis, warmly clad in leather coat, flying helmet and goggles. Always the organiser, he would mark out trials courses with bags of blue dye in the back of his Rolls. He was also credited with tackling many of the hair-raising Derbyshire trials sections on a Rolls-Royce chassis. Like more of us, Freddie rode in Derbyshire trials, and his favourite mount was a James V-twin and sidecar. In road racing he rode at many local circuits and raced in the TT during the years 1924 to 1929. Firstly on lightweight Rex Acme's, then a 350 James and finally on a 350 Velocette, which reputedly seized in mid-air at Ballaugh. On one occasion he was also said to have ended his race at Ballacraine by riding through the front door of the pub. For a year or two in the trials world around 1930 he ran the James team in the International Six Days Trial.

Freddie once 'borrowed' a Rolls-Royce chassis to collect a new James motorcycle from Birmingham for his own use, but the chassis was fitted with an experimental rear axle which broke down on the way. A desperate phone call to one of his mates in Derby produced the necessary replacements, and Freddie carried out the repairs at the side of the road. No one was any the wiser.

So when did he leave Rolls-Royce to start his own garage business in Derby? I have no definite date but would guess about 1925. He was the Derby agent for Rex Acme, James and Velocette. Those were glory years for Rex Acme with their ace rider Wal Handley, who was the first man to win two TTs in a week: the 1925 Ultra Lightweight and the Junior. Freddie and Wal were great friends.

Prior to that, the firm had lots of trouble with petrol tanks splitting, but Freddie devised a ball-and-socket arrangement which solved the problem. How did it work? Pass! No doubt there is an enthusiast out there who can tell us!

The Velocette team won the team prize in the 1928 Junior TT. Percy Goodman stands alongside Harold Willis, who came second on Roaring Anna, race winner Alec Bennett and Freddie Hicks, who came fifth. Harold Willis was the brilliant Velocette development engineer and wordsmith. His 'double knocker' for twin overhead camshaft is still in use today. So what happened to the machines that came first and second? Mr Velocette, Ivan Rhodes, owns them!

Prince Bira and Raymond Mays, both in ERAs, fight it out at the finish of the 1936 International Trophy at Brooklands. Only one second divided them after 250 racing miles, with Bira the winner.

Australian Alan Bruce took the world's maximum sidecar record from Germany's Ernst Henne at 123.15mph in 1932 on this 996cc supercharged Brough Superior.

Freddie knew Rolls-Royce premium apprentice Michael McEvoy and took him with him to the Isle of Man. Yes, he was the same Michael McEvoy who was later to start in business in Derby manufacturing McEvoy motorcycles.

During the 1920s Freddie had been a regular competitor at Syston Park, near Grantham, and he wondered if a similar circuit could be established near Derby. Looking around, he bought a ticket to Donington Park where the grounds were open to the public. Venturing away from the public area, he was investigating how two drives could be linked when he was challenged by an angry gamekeeper. Explaining why he was there, he was taken to see the owner, Justice of the Peace J.G. Shields.

Freddie explained his plan for a racing circuit near Derby, only to be told: 'Motorcycles – I hate them!' 'Yes,' replied Freddie 'you magistrates do, but if a race meeting brought 10,000 visitors into Donington you wouldn't mind, would you?' Mr Shields doubted this figure but Freddie, greatly daring, said he could guarantee it, so he was won over. The work to construct the circuit was immediately put in hand, and five weeks later, on Whit Monday 1932, the first meeting was held.

Freddie's vision was vindicated, and the crowd exceeded all expectations. At that time there was only one entrance off the road from Castle Donington to Kings Cliffe and the marshals on the gate were overwhelmed, eventually having to resort to collecting the money in wash hand basins. I knew the man, Alf Briggs of Derby, who won at that meeting and later met the man who won at the very first car meeting, driving a Bugatti that he had bought second hand for £150. Donington continued to greater successes, and the original circuit was improved and widened to permit car racing, culminating in the International Grand Prix in 1938 in which the all-conquering Auto Unions and Mercedes competed. As the secretary of the Derby Motor Club, Freddie was the unchallenged supremo at Donington and would brook no nonsense from anyone. No one was immune from his caustic tongue. On one occasion a rider on a water-cooled Scott was having trouble with his stubborn steed on the starting line when the impatient Freddie barked 'The eggs are boiled now, time to start!' If a rider was lagging behind, Freddie would say 'It's not the bike, it's the conductor!'

During the International Six Days Speed Trials at Donington in 1938 the formidable German 'Sports Fuehrer' wanted to be let onto the circuit with his car. 'I don't care if you're Adolf bloody Hitler,' said Freddie 'you're not going on the track'.

During car meetings, the rule was that at the end of a race cars had to be moved off the circuit to the paddock as soon as possible. After one race, which had been won by the great ERA driver Prince Bira, his car was left at the

Could this be 'The Little Rough 'un'? A famous Velocette racer which went through a number of hands, but in this photograph it is ridden by Cliff Ellesley from Lincolnshire. Basically it was a Mark V KTT with Mark IV fork blades, a Mark V bottom half and a KSS Mark Two head.

As I have already said, shortly after Chris and his family moved to Donington, he met Joe Hoult, who owned the 1930 ex-works Norton ridden by Stanley Woods. That was the year when the brand new Carroll-designed overhead camshaft Norton engine was introduced. This basic design was to continue through the 1930s and beyond World War Two. Joe had raced this machine in the 1932 Manx Grand Prix. He lived at Melbourne, about eight miles from Castle Donington, and had had a regular Sunday morning job when he took some people to attend church at Castle Donington. To fill in the time he would come to Chris's home for tea and biscuits. Joe and Chris would chat away about motorcycles, motorcycles, motorcycles, until it was time for Joe to pick up his passengers. Joe was great friends with Bob Vesey, and it was through Joe that Chris was able to buy Bob's 1924 Norton in 1934.

Chris would often ride over to visit Joe at Melbourne, and on the way he would pass over a 10ft-wide bridge over a stream. This required a quick left-right as he flew over. One day, as he did this, he heard a loud crack so he hastily slowed down. As he did so the flywheel parted as the crankpin had snapped, and this gave Chris his first lesson in metal fatigue. In May 1935, Joe Hoult sold Chris the Stanley Woods Norton for £50, so he then felt that he had a motorcycle suitable for competing at Donington.

Chris started to ride the Stanley Woods Norton on the road, and going round a bend at about 80mph he hit a bump on the road, the bike grounded and threw him across to the other side of the road, though still hanging on. If there had been any oncoming traffic he would have hit it, but fortunately the road was clear and after a couple of hops across the road he managed to regain control and got back to the correct side of the road. Chris then looked round the bike to see exactly what had happened. These Nortons were very low-slung, and with the bike heeled hard over the brake lever had hit the road and thrown the bike out of control. Chris ground away part of the brake lever at the point where it had hit the road. He went over to Norton's at Bracebridge

The great Jimmy Guthrie rides his works Norton in the 1935 Senior TT. He came second to Stanley Woods on the Guzzi by a matter of a few seconds but won the 350 Junior TT.

Harold Daniell, winner of the 1938 Senior TT and whose record lap was not equalled until 1950

Street, Birmingham, told them about his grounding problem and they, at no cost, found the longest fork spring they had in stock and gave it to him. Chris fitted it in the hope that it would help to solve the problem.

In 1936, Chris entered for the first meeting of the year at Donington. Although he lived at Donington and had been a regular spectator, he had never actually been round the circuit. So, one morning, Joe Hoult, with his then girlfriend, later his wife, took him to the park in his Wolseley Hornet (colloquially known as the Ice Cream Cornet). At that time the entry fee to get into the park was a shilling a person, so Joe told Chris to lie down in the back of the car, threw a blanket over him and saved a shilling. Joe drove him round the circuit, and they checked each corner for the camber, bend angle, surface etc and calculated the best line. Going towards Hollywood, they were doing about 40mph, and as they approached the open five-barred gate into the wood, Chris was sitting in the back of the car attempting to stamp on an imaginary brake pedal. It seemed to him that they were hurtling into a solid wall of trees, but he later found out that you could ride through this wooded section flat out in third, though he would often change into top to save the engine, despite the risk of grounding the rear brake lever.

For Chris's first race, he put in one of the three special copper electrode racing sparking plugs that Joe had given him, together with other bits and pieces when he bought the bike. He had never used these plugs before. The bike started up well enough, but when he opened the throttle it misfired badly, and for the first two laps it was splutter, splutter, bang, bang, so other riders were passing him quite easily. After that the misfiring cleared and he managed to finish a creditable fourth. He had resolved before the race that if he could not lap at 60mph he would not bother trying again. The lap record at that time was about 63mph. When the lap times were shown after the race he found that on the penultimate circuit he had achieved 60.11mph, so he was able to race again. There were never finals at Donington, they just took the heat times.

One night he was returning from Derby to Castle Donington on the Shardlow Straight where he had first seen Dusty riding flat out on his Ajay. Chris was travelling at about 70mph when he was passed by car with

The great Stanley Woods, whose inimitable style is clear in this photograph.

Freddie Frith, who became famous on Nortons and later on Velocettes.

tremendous headlights. Chris dropped down into third, opened the throttle and managed to pass the car before changing into top. At the end of the straight the car was on his heels, and looking round he could see a very shiny front axle running across the front of the car. It was a type 57 Bugatti, and he was to find later that it belonged to a Rolls-Royce premium apprentice named David Llewellyn Grifith Hughes. He became very friendly with David and still has a tyre pressure gauge, upon which he had stamped his initials 'DLGH'. David had discarded the gauge as faulty, but with a bit of work Chris got it working properly, and it still works to this day.

For his next race Chris had been working on the night shift at Rolls-Royce, so Joe collected him and took him to Donington. He did a few practice laps, but his first race was not until midday so the sensible thing to have done would have been to attempt to snatch an hour or two's rest. There was so much going on of compelling interest, however, that he failed to do so.

Chris was well back on the grid, and experience told him you could lose plenty of time when the flag went down. Some riders seemed almost casual in pushing their bikes off, and the odd ones who pushed their bikes from the right-hand side instead of the more usual left always seemed to get in your way.

Eventually he got going, and by the third lap he was well and truly clear of the backmarkers and beginning to catch up with the leaders. He came round the Craner Curves and caught up with a bunch of about six riders going very fast. He thought that he would get ahead of this lot without delay before what was then called the old hairpin. It was a sharp right-hand, almost a right-angle bend, and with a pronounced rise as you rounded it. The other riders started to slow down well before the corner so Chris, remembering Bob Vesey, kept the throttle open, passed them, braked late and got round the corner smartly, but when the bike landed after a slight bump the gearbox pivot bolt hit the ground and Chris was thrown off. Chris slid along the grass, but his bike bounced along the track and got somewhat

The great Norton rider 'Crasher' White rides in the 1937 German Grand Prix. Riding to orders, he finished second behind Harold Daniell.

The spring frame first fitted to works Nortons in 1936.

battered. The bars were bent, petrol tank dented and the filler spout of the oil tank was knocked off. Chris later 'repaired' the oil filler, but from then on he had to use the blanking cap on the right-hand side as distinct from the original filler spout. August came and he entered again. He was delighted when he won his heat, and a little later he was in the same heat as Austin Munks who had won several Manx Grand Prix races. In 1935 Austin had lost an eye in a shooting accident, but now he had recovered enough to ride at Donington, though everyone was sorry for him and would have made every effort not to get in his way. He wore a bandage across his missing eye and had an odd-looking Velocette which Chris later realised was a Mark V KTT, known by the Velocette works as 'The little rough 'un'. On the grid everyone made way for Austin. Down came the flag, and off went Austin with all the other riders chasing him. Chris remembers going round the

Craner Curves and seeing Austin disappear under the stone bridge a couple of hundred yards ahead of him. Chris was lying in about fourth or fifth place when it started to rain heavily, so knowing that the track through the woods was very slippery in the wet and having just won his heat he decided to take it easy rather than risk falling off. He finished ninth in that heat, which was not bad when you consider the class of people who rode at Donington.

A typical Donington entry list would include, in addition to those mentioned: Wal Handley, Jimmy Simpson (who did not do well on his only appearance), Harold Daniel, Freddie Frith, Stanley Woods, Tyrell Smith, Les Graham, Ken Bills, Jock West and many other famous riders. One of the most spectacular sights that Chris remembers was seeing Walter Rusk on the supercharged, four-cylinder, water-cooled AJS which weaved around like a drunken sailor! Jimmy Guthrie was about the only star he did not remember riding at Donington. Maurice Cann, winner of the 1937 Senior and Junior Manx Grand Prixs, was a regular. Post-war he won several Ulsters and one Lightweight TT.

Chris was once in the same heat as Harold Daniel, the man who won the 1938 TT and set a lap record of 91mph that was to remain unbroken until 1950. Once the flag went down, Chris never saw Harold again. Riding at Donington, Chris was never lapped, though he lapped plenty of other people. He says it was a lot easier to pass a good rider on a bend because you knew exactly what line he was going to take. The rabbits, however, were liable to dart anywhere.

After winning his heat, a fellow rider with a 500cc Norton came across to chat to him. He worked at Rolls-Royce, and when Chris told him that he had always wanted to work there he, to Chris's surprise, said that he could get him a job in the machine shop. Chris decided there and then that he would abandon being a staff member at Celanese and become a driller at Rolls-Royce.

Chapter 13

HOSPITAL

O n his way to work from Donington, Chris would pass the Bridge Inn at Shardlow. On many Monday mornings one of George Brough's bikes, or sometimes cars, would be parked outside as George had obviously spent the night there. Chris never saw him arrive or leave but, reputedly, the landlady was his lady friend. George's Brough Superior factory in Nottingham, only half an hour's ride from Chris's home at Castle Donington, was very scruffy by comparison with the beautiful bikes that it turned out.

Before Bob Vesey was killed he had ridden from Derby to Skegness, a good 100 miles, in a one hour 45 minutes, so Chris thought he would see if he could equal that. On 30 August 1936 he set out from home with his mother checking that the time was exactly 6.35am as he left the front door. By 8.20am he was in Skegness on the promenade by the clock tower when he asked a passer-by to sign his diary to confirm the time and was very proud that he had equalled Bob's time.

On the run over he was on a long, straight section of road with no hedges either side when he thought that the Norton was slowing. He tried to open the throttle wider, only to realise that he was already flat out. He remembered Bob's advice that it was that last bit of throttle that did the damage so he rolled the throttle back a bit. Had he been on a tree-lined road he would have realised how fast he was going!

Three days after this on Sunday 16 August Chris caught up with a rider of a 350cc Excelsior Manxman. They both had pillion riders, so Chris took him on and left him. As they slowed for a small town they came to a side turning and the Excelsior rider turned down into it. Chris did a quick U-turn, foolishly caught him up, then proceeded to show him how to ride round country lane corners. The road was only about 12ft wide, so Chris passed him and rounded the next corner, only to find a car parked some yards ahead, and side by side with it was another car coming towards him on the wrong side of the road. The road was completely blocked, so Chris slammed on the brakes and remembers no more.

Chris later met the Excelsior rider, who told him what had happened next. Apparently the bike went down and both Chris and his passenger went sliding down the road when they tried to knock a brick wall down with their heads! There were no crash hats in those days, remember. The Manxman also went down so all four of them were lying on the road. The car drivers and passengers all anxiously jumped out of their cars to check on their condition as Chris and his pillion passenger were unconscious and bleeding from their heads, but the other two got back on their feet and after staggering about a bit seemed okay. The Manxman pillion rider had only one arm, but among all the blood and dust the car passengers, becoming almost hysterical, assumed that it had been chopped off in the crash and had gone missing.

'The Rolls-Royce of Motorcycles' said the manufacturer, George Brough. This is one of the top-of-the-range SS100s.

The Excelsior Manxman was one of the prettiest and most purposeful motorcycles of all time. This is the 250cc version.

The next thing Chris remembers was that it was getting dark and he was asking where his bike was. He was told that the bike was fine and not to worry about it. He must have then lost consciousness again because the next thing he remembers was that it was dark, the ambulance had arrived and he was being loaded onto it. He remembered nothing about his pillion passenger but was greatly relieved when they arrived at Derby and the ambulance stopped at some traffic lights. He realised that they must be near the Derbyshire Royal Infirmary, and when he got there a competent and well-endowed nurse put his head on her bosom and pulled his scalp, which had apparently been torn back, into position. He never felt a thing! His mother came to see him, but his father said 'Well, if he is silly enough to get himself into hospital he can stay there!'

Eventually Chris was well enough to be sent home, and his mother brought a bed downstairs for him rather than having to cope with him in his usual attic bedroom. He had quite a few visitors, including Cherry Parsons. After some days of rest he was finally able to get back on his feet and all was well.

Soon after that, Ian Findlay came to see Chris. He was a fanatical motorcycle enthusiast and a great friend of Maurice Patey. To us he was always

'Pate's mate Findlay'. Chris still had the 1924 Model 18 Norton on which he had lost his licence, so Ian bought it and, would you believe it, finished second in the first vintage race they ever had at Donington in 1939. Ian was a keen member of the Vintage Motorcycle Club, and one of the sections ran an Ian Findlay Memorial event after he died. He had attended a Vintage Motorcycle Club meeting, and when it was over he went out, got into his car, had a heart attack and died.

Chris, as previously mentioned, had an attic bedroom and would frequently arrive home well after 10pm when the Castle Donington street gas lights were dimmed. There was no electric light in the attic room so a candle was the only option, but Chris did not bother about any lighting and would usually go straight to bed. In the evenings, looking out of the window, he would often see the village policeman standing on the opposite corner having a sly fag, which he hid in his hand but if he happened to be lighting up it was plain to see.

Their family house was called Hilltop and was set back from the road, so you had to go up a ramp to get to it. When arriving home late, he was anxious to avoid waking the neighbours so he would ride quietly up the hill, turn off the petrol, go past the house, then do a 180-degree turn at the bottom of nearby Park Lane. He would then snap the throttle open to stall the engine

A late 1930s 500cc Rudge Ulster.

95

Wal Handley, one of the all-time greats, only rode works Nortons in 1934. Here he is in his last road race rocketing over Balloo Bridge on the seven-mile Clady straight in the Ulster Grand Prix. He was killed flying in World War Two.

and coast back downhill with enough speed to ride onto the path at the adjacent Moira pub, thence up the ramp to his home.

The village policeman, after seeing this a few times, worked out that Chris's brakes were no good as he was unable to stop at his home. He stopped Chris and demanded a brake check; however, when Chris demonstrated that the policeman could not push the bike while Chris had one finger on the front brake lever and had explained what he was up to, all was well. In October Chris decided to weigh the Norton and confirmed the weight at 316lb. The current Manx Nortons could whistle past Chris on acceleration so he decided to reduce the weight wherever possible. He drilled the brake levers, engine plates, clutch plates, and cut away the clutch housing. He also drilled the flywheels but the Norton was never a match on acceleration for the mid-

1930s racing bikes. Once flat out, the other riders only went past slowly, but when accelerating they continued to whistle past him. He also realised that the current 350cc racing Rudges, of which there seemed to be plenty, were also faster than him down the straight.

In January 1937, with the Norton only used for racing, Chris bought a 500cc Rudge Special to use on the road, but this seemed a ponderous device after the Norton.

At the Donington Easter meeting he snapped his front brake lever, probably as a result of changing down with the front brake hard on. He carried on but found that it had knocked 3mph off his lap times. Borrowing the front brake lever off another bike, he rocketed away in the next heat until, going through the woods towards Coppice Lodge, the Norton seized. On taking off the head and barrel he found that he had mis-fitted a plate from under the barrel, which

Austin Munks riding to victory on his KTT Mark V Velocette in the 1936 Junior Manx Grand Prix, despite losing an eye in a shooting accident.

had a hole in it coinciding with an oilway to feed the back of the piston, so he had inadvertently blanked off the oil supply.

One night, Chris was riding home along a dark lane at a modest speed but with only his dim battery lights for illumination when he passed a pedestrian, and immediately after a little white dog ran from his offside, missing the front wheel but hitting the side of the bike. He suspected that the man had called the dog which had darted across the road rather than simply darting at the machine.

Chris was sorry for the poor little thing but could not see that there was any point in stopping so he proceeded at his minimum top gear speed. But the first time he tried to change gear he found that he could not. The gear lever was still there, so he proceeded along steadily in top gear. Investigation revealed that the external mechanism for this early positive stop gear-change mechanism, which had a main pivot bolt, was all missing as the bolt had snapped. Next day he went back to the spot where he had hit the dog hoping to see if he could find any of the pawls and ratchets but could not find a thing so had to buy them all.

Chapter 14

STARTING AT ROLLS-ROYCE

Dennis Jones worked for Rolls-Royce, and he was a superlative motorcycle engineer. Dennis designed and manufactured a number of motorcycles, including overhead camshaft 250 singles, four-cylinder overhead camshaft machines and a four-cylinder supercharged two stroke. This, remember, was in the 1930s, so Dennis was an engineer far ahead of his time. Dennis and Chris were great friends and I also knew Dennis.

In June that year, Dennis asked Chris to take him to Burton, where he picked up a 1934 OK Supreme that Ginger Wood had ridden in the 1934 TT.

Racing at Donington in August, Chris caught up with Cherry Parsons who was riding his 1935 Manx Norton. This was at Coppice Lodge, and Chris decided that if he left his braking until very late he would be able to pass Cherry then see how far he could get along the straight before Cherry inevitably passed him. All went as planned until Chris took his foot of the brake, only to find that the brake stayed on. The problem was that with worn linings all was fine when the drum was cold, but when it expanded due to the heat generated by braking the brake cam went further round and stuck. The locked back wheel spun round and threw Chris off, narrowly missing Cherry's rear wheel. When Chris managed to stand up he thought he had sprained his right wrist.

Race over, he fired up the Norton, rode carefully to the paddock and after the end of the meeting he rode the bike home. The pain in his wrist meant that he got little sleep that night and the same again the night after,

A tidy 350cc side-valve Humber of the 1920s, though Chris's Humber would have been a later model.

so at last he had to give in and go to the doctor, who took one look at the wrist and sent him for an X-ray.

This revealed a broken scaphoid, so his wrist was bent back at right angles to his fore-arm and plastered in that position. This meant that he could not use the clutch lever, so he turned it round 180 degrees so that it faced backwards instead of forwards and he could then manage to operate it by pressing on it with his palm. With that set-up, he managed to run, bump and jump on successfully, and, although clumsy, the clutch action was quite light and he never once 'lost' the bike. Once aboard, it was no problem, and he rode it like that for eight weeks.

He could not, of course, operate his drilling machine 'one-handed', and in trying to find an alternative job he came to the attention of Mr Vale who was in charge of the Rolls-Royce aero-engine machine shop. His son had been at Derby school with Chris, so he remembered him gaining awards in 1931 and 1932. He found Chris a job in production control, and although he did quite well there he wanted to get a more 'hands on' job.

Works manager Harry Swift eventually offered him a job on his staff. Fortunately, by then, Rio Mirza was working at Rolls-Royce, and with his help Chris got a job on the experimental test-beds, which was just the kind of thing he wanted.

As he did not want to ride the Norton through the winter, he bought a 1928 Humber for about a fiver. It was a bit rough and on looking inside the engine, he found that someone had welded up a hole in the crown of the piston. They had left a very large, crude lump on the crown but after a bit of tidying up he put the whole thing back. When he replaced the badly worn valves and guides, however, he found that the replacement valves could not bed properly onto the seats. After much hard work scraping, he finally managed to get a good enough seal to get some compression back.

Riding home on the Norton one night, he realised that the rear tyre was nearly flat so he moved up to sit on the front of the tank and proceeded slowly home, but about four miles before he got there the protesting tyre burst, resulting in a bit of swervery, but fortunately he managed to stay aboard.

The 1938 500cc BMW was one of the most desirable machines of its era, though Chris was not very impressed!

Freddie Frith lands at 100mph at the top of Bray Hill in the 1938 TT. He finished third, less than two seconds behind Stanley Woods. The race winner was Harold Daniel, whose record lap of 91mph was not equalled until 1950.

In September, Rio Mirza bought a new R51 BMW. This was very sporty, with twin Brooklands silencers, and when he came to visit Chris he was offered a ride on it which, of course, he was delighted to accept. Being used to the Norton's lusty exhaust beat, however, the BMW seemed to be revving its heart out at 60mph, so he felt no desire to go any faster.

Chapter 15

RACING AT CADWELL PARK

In 1938, Chris rode at Cadwell Park to settle in the Norton before Donington. In the Folbigg Trophy he qualified in his heat for the final but noticed on the last bend that the Norton, unusually, wagged its head. Back in the pits he found that the steering damper anchorage to the tank top had broken. Foolishly, with the Final coming up, he decided to race without the damper, but on the starting grid the Norton, with more sense than its rider, spat back and Chris was last off.

'I'll soon catch these riders,' thought Chris, so he roared up the hill immediately after the start and laid the bike hard over into the bend at the top. The bike immediately went into a tank slapper, and Chris's only choice was to jump off. He rolled and bounced on the grass straight into a single large tree around which someone had thoughtfully wrapped a mattress. He clouted it full on then fell to the ground unconscious.

A doctor came along and asked the usual questions. He was badly bruised, but what worried him most was that on his first contact with the ground, sliding sideways, he landed on the trailing side of his backside and, of course, the leading half wanted to carry on at 60mph so he thought that he had done himself a serious mischief! As it turned out, however, it was nothing serious. Years later, the widow of one of his old friends got in touch with him to say that she had been there at the time and had seen the whole thing.

On the following Monday he was due to ride at Donington but had very little sleep and was aching all over. Looking at the programme, however, he felt that he could win the first heat – and a heat won is always a positive start. He

Charles Markham of *Motor Cycling*. There was only George Brough who could wear a cap like Charles Markham!

was well placed on the grid, got off to a good start and was away in the lead. Into a bend, braking hard and banking well over, he was sideswiped by a newcomer to Donington who was quite unprepared for Chris's racing line.

Chris was bowled off, winded and shaken. He lost a foot-rest among other damage, so after the race he went over to the pits, found the offender and used all the bad language he could think of. The other rider, however, was most apologetic and took no offence. He even offered to lend Chris his bike for the rest of the day, but Chris was in no mood or condition to ride again so he turned down the offer. With hindsight, Chris regrets the way he spoke to the other rider and lost the opportunity to do so when he was killed in the 1946 Manx Grand Prix.

Chapter 16

WORK AT ROLLS-ROYCE TAKES PRIORITY

In March 1939 Chris sold the Norton. Working as a leading hand experimental aero-engine tester at Rolls-Royce, he was working up to 80 hours a week, evenings and weekends, so there was no way he could have hoped to race at Donington. He thought, however, that he might find time to do a bit of grass-tracking or scrambling so he bought a Scott for everyday use with a view to putting a side-car chassis on it if he ever found a suitable grass-tracker.

Shortly afterwards the right bike turned up: a 1930 350cc racing Raleigh with a spare dope piston from the great Derby rider, Alf Briggs. The bike had raced successfully on the Continent, and his friend Alf had raced it with great success both locally and at Cadwell. Chris handed over the purchase price of £15 and was asked not to start it up there as the neighbours would complain about the open exhaust.

After Chris got the bike home he pushed it up and down the road for about 10 minutes with never a bleep. He changed the plugs etc but still no start. He now wondered why Alf had asked him not to attempt to start up and annoy the neighbours. He removed and dismantled the racing BTH magneto, put the armature in his mother's oven, gently warmed it for an hour so, cleaned everything up, re-assembled it and the bike started right away.

A 1930 350cc Racing Raleigh.

He then took it to his first scramble which, to his astonishment, he managed to win. It was some years since he had abandoned speedway-type riding, but the technique obviously came back to him. He later raced it on grass-tracks and was delighted to achieve an occasional win.

Riding the Scott to a meeting with the Raleigh on the chassis, he was riding along a straight at about 50mph when he came to a corner. Solo he could have got round it at over 70mph, but having forgotten the sidecar he attempted a gentle bank to the left. The bike, of course, ignored him and carried straight on to the right-hand kerb. The outfit mounted the kerb and hurtled onto a wide, smooth grass verge which gave Chris time to wake up and regain control. Fortunately there was no oncoming traffic.

In August he was scrambling on a very bumpy track and the long-wheelbase Raleigh started to buck. The front wheel dug into a steep rise and over the top went Chris. He found that he had a sore thumb as he must have banged it back quite hard, and it hurt for several weeks. After the war he got a touch of arthritis in that thumb, and after an X-ray the doctor asked him when he had broken it. Obviously that was in 1939, and there was a well-rounded piece of bone which, the doctor assured him, must have been there since then!

Going to another meeting, he was climbing a steep hill on the well-laden Scott outfit when it blew a head gasket. The radiator filler cap was specially

A 1930 Scott TT Replica.

designed with a little vent so that the resultant jet of hot water hit you straight in the face. All good clean fun. He learned to change gear in the time-honoured Scott manner by using his left hand to reach over the tank to the right-hand gear-change lever without using the clutch when changing up.

One moonlight night he remembers riding the Scott halfway home and thinking how very quiet and smooth it was when he realised he had his ear-plugs, always used on the test-beds, still in his ears!

War broke out in September 1939, so he needed something more economical than the 596cc TT replica Scott. He always thought that it was about as much TT as my aunt Sally! He bought an early 1930s 250cc JAP-engined OK Supreme, which had dynamo lighting and four speeds so it was very good for economic to-and-from-work transport. Using thousands of gallons of 100 octane aviation fuel on the test rigs, little bottles of it frequently found their way past the watchmen and into their tanks, but there was one character who used to fill up 5 gallon drums of a 100 octane fuel and put them in the boot of his car on a regular basis. Chris eventually stopped him doing this as it could have got all of them into trouble, but he was obviously very resentful when they forced him to take the 5 gallon drums out of the boot of his car and put the fuel back in the tanks where it belonged.

The great Walter Rusk with the 250cc overhead camshaft OK Supreme he raced in the 1938 Lightweight TT. No, not the same as Chris's bread and butter two-fifty!

One day riding back home Chris looked behind him for some reason and thought it was funny that he had not noticed the trail of oil on the road. He stopped the bike and looked ahead to see if it also extended ahead as well as behind. He then realised that the oil was coming from his bike so he walked back and was fortunate to find the sump plug at the beginning of the oil trial. He would have bet a fair sum of money on guessing the identity of the person who had loosened the sump plug and left it on one thread!

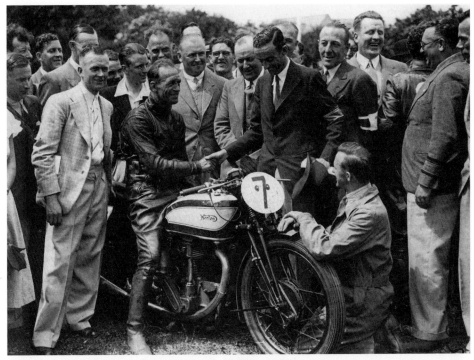

Jimmy Guthrie is congratulated on winning the 1936 Senior TT.

Jimmy Guthrie and Freddie Frith prepare their works 350 Nortons at Berne in 1937. They finished first and second in the 350 and 500 classes.

One winter's night he had worked up to midnight and was riding steadily home in a snowstorm. There had been a car or two through the snow, and he was riding along one of the car tracks, probably too fast for those conditions. He got into a front-wheel skid and ended up lying on the road with the OK on top of him. His leg was trapped under the bike, and he could not extract himself from it. There had been a thaw and re-freeze which meant that there was a layer of ice under the snow, and he could not find anything to push against. He wondered if he was either going to spend the night there or remain trapped until a car ran over him, but after what seemed like an age, though was probably only a few minutes, he managed to get himself clear and was off home.

In 1940 the war was going very badly, so he decided that he would like to join up, despite being in a reserved occupation, so this brings us to the end of his pre-war motorcycling days and to next stage of the Chris Harrison story.

The Rolls-Royce Kestrel first ran on test in December 1926 and was considerably upgraded. Finally in 1938 fully supercharged versions produced 640hp at 1,000ft and 2,700rpm. It was fitted to many different types of aircraft and in service in World War Two.

The final development of the Kestrel was the completely modernised version of 1937, which was called the Peregrine. Many of its features were based on the Merlin, which was already being developed. It produced 885hp at 3,000rpm and 15,000ft.

The Vulture was an ambitious design started in September 1935. It was a 24-cylinder engine of X configuration using Kestrel cylinder blocks: virtually two engines, one upright and the other inverted below it. A massive 42.48 litres, 1,845hp at 3,000rpm and 5,000ft, it was never completely successful and was superseded by the Merlin.

The Griffon started life in 1934 with intensive development from January 1939 and was, in effect, a de-tuned version of the R engine with the same 26.7-litre capacity. It was the 'big brother' of the Merlin, though not that much more powerful. A very successful engine, towards the end of the war they were producing 2,340hp at low level. Chris ran all these engines, except the R engine, on test, and the author worked on Merlin and Griffon development.

The origin of the Griffon was the amazing Rolls-Royce 'R' racing engine, V-12, 36.7 litres. It was designed to win the Schneider Trophy, an international seaplane contest. The 1927 event was won by a seaplane designed by the great R.J. Mitchell, who was later to design the Spitfire, and powered by a Napier Lion engine. The 1929 event was won by another Mitchell-designed seaplane powered by the R engine. For the 1931 event the Government could not justify the £100,000 required to develop the engine further to produce the extra power required to win the trophy, so ex-actress Lady Houston stepped forward with £100,000 of her own money and said 'Every Briton would rather sell his last shirt than admit that England could not afford to defend herself against all comers'. The target power was 2,300hp, and no engine made by man had ever before exceeded one hp for each cubic inch of capacity. A superhuman effort by the RR development team produced 2,360hp to win the trophy for all time in Mitchell's seaplane.

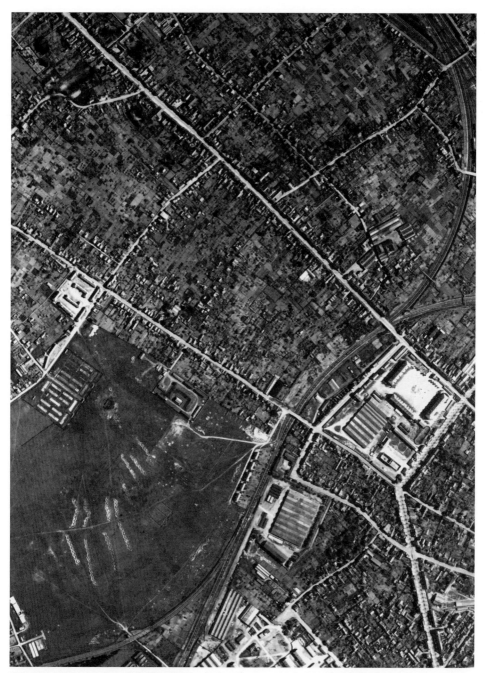

This photograph is of an airfield in France before the invasion taken by Derby Mosquito pilot George Watson and his navigator. It was no longer in use, but ditches had been dug to prevent use by possible invading forces.

This aerial photograph of Caen just before the invasion was taken by the same pilot and navigator.

Chapter 17

CHRIS JOINS THE RAF

After the retreat from Dunkirk, Chris began to think that he should be doing something more active to assist the war effort. His work, as a leading hand experimental aero-engine tester at Rolls-Royce, meant that he could not be called-up but could volunteer. When Rolls-Royce realised this he was offered various jobs, but he explained that he did not want to service aircraft but would rather fly them. He went down to Derby Town Hall to volunteer for service in the RAF and then was sent back to Rolls-Royce awaiting call-up. When his call-up papers arrived he was told to report to Cardington in Bedfordshire, where the huge hangars stood that were built for the construction of the airship R101.

He and his colleagues were sworn in and issued with uniforms. They were then posted to an Initial Training Wing Number 11 at Scarborough, and there they spent eight weeks doing basic training. They were then posted to the US, sailing from Liverpool in the French ship the *Louis Pasteur* which had been towed out of the Mediterranean, had all necessarily work completed and was then released as a troop transport. They were accompanied by an aircraft carrier due for servicing and four of the four-stacker destroyers supplied by America under lend lease. After a number of days, the convoy arrived in Canada, the troops disembarked and were sent by train to Maxwell Field, Montgomery, Alabama. They then found, to their disgust, that they were required to undergo, yet again, their initial training. This time it was the American version, but they had joined up to learn to fly, not to carry a rifle on the wrong shoulder, salute in a different manner and do the initial training all over again!

Chris gets his wings as Duty Flight Leader.

Following afternoon training, all eight squadrons had to parade on the airfield and then march off to music played by an American military band. On arrival at the dining hall they were subjected to reports as to how they had performed on the march. At the first of such events, when one of the squadrons was listed as the best, the others all signified their disapproval of this verdict. Although this was obviously a light-hearted protest, the Americans did not understand this and thought that it reflected very badly upon them, so this never happened again.

Chris shakes hands with fellow pupil Derek Sharpe sitting in a Stearman. Sadly he was killed flying over Germany in 1942.

One day the band struck up *Colonel Bogey* and somebody in Chris's Squadron quietly sang the somewhat coarse British words to the music. Before long they were all bellowing '*****s and the same to you' though still marching very smartly. When they got to the dining hall they expected a reprimand but, to their surprise, they were congratulated on their high morale! Even so, they were fairly sure that the Americans only later realised what they had been singing.

Shortly after this the troops' disgruntled attitude must have reached the ears of Hughie Edwards VC, one of the four or five highly decorated pilots who had been with them on the *Louis Pasteur* and had accompanied them to

Maxwell Field. They were assembled in a large hangar and had the opportunity to let him know their opinion. He then spoke to them of the great service that the US was rendering to Britain, and it was their responsibility to realise that. From then on they decided to behave themselves and not make any more waves. They then happily sat at 'attention' in the dining hall, began to eat at the correct moment, stopped eating at the command 'rest' but remained seated regardless of what was left on their plates at the command of 'attention'.

After eight weeks of this, they were posted to Miami, Oklahoma, where there was a grass aerodrome and they were taught to fly the Stearman, a rather robust biplane. These planes are still flying today.

During Chris's training, fellow student Derek Sharpe got into his Stearman but failed to fasten his safety harness. His instructor went into a loop and poor Derek shot out of the plane, but by a miracle he landed on the rear of the fuselage, facing backwards, so he was able to hang onto the tail fin. The pilot managed to control the tail-heavy Stearman and landed safely. Within hours, however, reporters and photographers from all over the United States appeared and it was big news. Sadly Derek was killed in action flying over occupied Europe in 1942.

May 1941. The Germans ignore their pact and invade Russia. Why did Hitler make such a disastrous error? Napoleon had made the same mistake over a century earlier.

Pearl Harbor, 7 December 1941, when 360 Japanese war planes made a surprise attack on the US Pacific Fleet and brought the United States into the war.

The trainee pilots had in charge of them a World War One Flight Lieutenant named Grimes and, of course, he was the nearest thing to God as far as LAC Harrison was concerned. Some of the previous pupils had gone hitchhiking at weekends, and having arrived at New York or Los Angeles they found they had trouble getting back in time, so Grimes had ordered that no one could leave the State which, as far as Chris could see, was not going to worry him.

Naturally, Chris kept contact with his friends at Rolls-Royce and was intrigued when one of them wrote to him. It was the same Alf Poyser who had been the experimental representative who had attended all the world-record attempts by Rolls-Royce including the Schneider Trophy races. He was now at Packards, Detroit, who were just starting Rolls-Royce Merlin production. When Chris replied he wrote saying 'Would you believe it, I am in America too!' The reply he received was quite unexpected and told him that

A Curtiss P-40 'Flying Tiger'.

The Chance Vought Corsair, which was the first US fighter of any type to exceed 400mph in level flight; 404mph was achieved in 1940.

he was to go to Packards as soon as possible. Naturally, he wrote back to say that he was not allowed to leave Alabama and thought that would be the end of the matter; however, in a few days he got a letter telling him to advise Flight Lieutenant Grimes that if he would not allow Chris to go to Detroit, Washington would order him to!

But there lay the problem. How did LAC Harrison tell God, sorry, Grimes, something like that? After much thought, however, he plucked up courage, went to see Grimes and told him that he had been asked to go to Detroit. 'Permission denied. Dismissed!' came the reply. Chris thought that Grimes could, at least, have asked why he was expected to go to Detroit and so, plucking up his courage again, he mumbled to the effect that if he did not send him, Washington would tell him to.

Well, that blew it! Chris was the worst aircraftman that Grimes had ever met. One more word from him, and he would be on a charge. Chris hastily got out of the office, and when his hands were steady enough he wrote to Poyser to explain the position. Then, sure that that would be the end of the matter, he decided to forget all about it and get on with learning to fly.

Some days later there was a call for LAC Harrison to report to Flight Lieutenant Grimes. Wondering what he had done wrong, Chris hastened to Grimes's office. On entering, Grimes just pushed some papers across the desk to him and announced: 'You are going to Detroit.' Chris bit his tongue, refrained from saying 'I told you so', left the office and caught the next available train to Detroit.

Chapter 18

CHRIS STARTS WORK AT PACKARD, DETROIT

On his arrival at the Packard factory in Detroit, Chris was escorted round every section of the factory by the head of each section for the first three days. As Chris was fully experienced in Merlin manufacture at Derby there was much for him to comment upon, and these comments were obviously reported to Mr George Christopher, the chief executive. On the fourth day he was ushered into Mr Christopher's office.

He found Mr Christopher to be a very pleasant person, and after some preliminary discussion he said that he had not got Chris to come to Detroit just for a guided tour of the Packard factory. Chris replied that he realised that he was expected to come and work at Packards but, somewhat tactlessly, he said that all they were doing was producing a marque that he had type-tested about two years earlier. He went on to say that despite having spent the last two years working on subsequent types of Merlins, he had decided that he wanted to fly rather work on the ground.

Mr Christopher displayed no irritation at Chris's attitude, and after some further conversation about Merlin manufacture he casually asked how many students were there in Alabama learning to fly. Chris replied that there must be several hundred. Christopher then asked that, if one less pilot arrived in England but the result was more engines for their planes, might that be a good idea? Chris had to agree. So he somewhat reluctantly agreed that he would

"The price of petrol has been increased by one penny."—Official.

March 1942. This dramatic cartoon by Philip Zec in the *Daily Mirror* signalled the end of the basic petrol ration. Until then, a small amount of petrol had been allowed for private use, but all petrol came from America, and the tankers were prime targets for the German U-boats. When the basic ration ended there was no more private motoring or motorcycling for the rest of the war.

come to Packards for six months. Before he was summoned to Packards he had finished his primary course and gone solo on the low-wing monoplane 'basic'Vultee B13. On his arrival in Packards in mid-March 1941 he was kitted out in civilian clothes and started work. He was based on the 28 production beds but had access to all departments. As the factory was working a three-shift 24-hour day, when he started his shift he could liaise with Poyser and then again before he left at 5.30pm. He would then check any problems that might have arisen in production, staying until after midnight, if necessary, to talk to the follow-up shift.

Packards had a system of awards in its 'Work-to-win' programme consisting of gold and diamond pendants for any outstanding efforts. Chris was awarded three of these but subsequently lost them all. One of them was for solving a problem with the supercharger speed change mechanism. Mid-evening production were given a new set of operating forks but found that they could not be installed using the available limits. Chris spent some time trying out all the possibilities and was able to give the section a set of figures with which they could work until next morning arrived, and it was possible to contact Derby to get the official figures. This saved a 12-hour delay that would have meant eight or 10 less engines on the assembly line.

Very few Englishmen had visited America before the war, so for these young RAF men it was amazing cultural experience. They had seen it all, of

July 1942. Rommel is halted at last at El Alamein. Up to then Rommel, 'The Desert Fox', had appeared to be invincible, but Alamein finally turned the tide.

course, in the American films of the day but never in real life. Chris bought a Ford V-8 and was able to see something of the country, and he even experienced the social barrier the existed between black and white which was, of course, non-existent in England. He made the most of his time there. He got on very well with his fellow workers despite, on occasion, being called 'The Limey'. He made many friends, one of whom lived in a house that he had made out of flattened oil drums! He was a huge man who raced a Doodle Bug, which was a tiny little racing car that competed on cinder tracks, rather like British speedway motorcycle racing but with these tiny cars instead. After the war he came over to Europe and raced Ferraris.

One day Chris was asked to investigate a leak on a Merlin crankcase and found that the mechanic had prised off the cover plate with a screwdriver, bruising and possibly scraping the crankcase. Chris was understandably furious, but soon afterwards one of the union men came to see him indignantly asking why the Limey was abusing one of his men. When Chris explained what had happened and the possible results he castigated his own unionist telling him that such ham-fisted methods were totally unacceptable, and if they continued he would be out of the union and out of a job!

Turning this affair to his own advantage, Chris asked if he, too, could join the union, and when the answer was 'Why not?' he promptly joined. From then on, whenever Chris wanted something done 'The Rolls-Royce way', he would simply produce his union badge and threaten to call the convenor to back him up.

One of his journeys with the Ford V-8 was to visit the relatives of a Castle Donington family who lived in Canada just over the border from Detroit. As Chris was a British citizen he thought that getting into Canada would be no problem at all, but on arriving at the border without any paperwork to validate his presence in Detroit it was suspected that he was a British deserter trying to get into Canada. He was put in a small room and questioned for hours before he could convince them exactly why he was in Detroit. By the time he was released, however, it was too late to go over to Canada, but he was subsequently issued with a certificate to say that he was in the US 'On a military mission.'

Work went on well, and his six months were up surprisingly quickly. When he pointed out, however, that he was supposed to be returning to flying it seemed that Packard and the British Air Commission had decided otherwise. He was told that they were very pleased with him and that he was doing a good job, but after much discussion he was finally released following a further three months' work.

Chapter 19

BACK TO FLYING TRAINING

After he left Detroit, Chris was not sent back to the US Army Air Corps in Alabama but instead went straight back to to No.3 British Flying Training School in Miami, Oklahoma. In Miami his CO was Wing Commander Roxborough with whom Chris got on very well indeed. He went back to primary training and finished the course flying a low-wing monoplane, the Percival Prentice. He next flew the AT6A, known in the UK as the Harvard.

He completed the course with no problems, and after the final school exams he was rated third out of over 80 students. He was then commissioned. The student who came first was an ex-ground crew Sergeant, and the second was USAAC Corps Sergeant, who was one of about half a dozen Americans on the course, so Chris considered that his third place was a very satisfactory result.

Following his commission, Chris returned to Britain via Canada on the *Louis Pasteur*, dodging U-boats on what was a nerve-wracking trip! On the way into Liverpool they passed several war-damaged wrecks. He was next brought before a selection panel, where Chris expressed his preference for night fighters. Posted to Grantham, he learned to fly Blenheims. One of his fellow students was an Australian pilot officer named Miller who had played cricket for Australia with Don Bradman. Chris is under the impression that he eventually flew Mosquitos.

Chris was next posted to Charter Hall near Berwick-on-Tweed, and after some dual instruction on Beauforts, there being no dual Beaufighters, he flew solo on a Merlin-engined Beau II.

Stanford Hall. Chris in the saddle of M.D. Whitworth's Rex Acme, which managed 90mph at Brooklands. Derby racing man Alf Briggs is on the left, and Tich Allan, founder of the Vintage Motorcycle Club, is on the right.

Derbyshire's Ivan Rhodes, the world's leading authority on Velocettes, with his equally talented son, Grahame. They are standing behind 'The Roarer', a twin-cylinder, supercharged, shaft-drive Velocette made for the 1939 TT but never raced. It was one of the most desirable motorcycles of all time. All the engine internals went missing during the war but were painstakingly manufactured by Ivan and Grahame.

The rebuilt 1924 model.

The rebuilt 1927 model.

This incomplete tangle of rusty rubbish are the remains of 1924 and 1927 Round Tank BSA's. Chris did not just restore them, he reconstructed them!

An early 1920s V-twin BSA. Back when the world was young, the author and his friend Harry 'T' Tunaley left Rolls-Royce to start in the motorcycle business. A 1927 770cc sidecar version was their workhorse. The sidecar body was exchanged for a flat wooden platform with a post at either end and used to transport everything from motorcycles to steel girders.

Chris with the author's 1922 Bullnose Morris.

A miniature version of the racing C-type Jaguar made by Watsonian Sidecars. This is one of the Earls Court Show models bought for the author's daughter, Caroline. It was originally fitted with a Villiers four-stroke engine, but Chris is shown here fitting a self-start Honda 50 engine.

Children's version of the 1930s Austin Seven racer driven brilliantly at Brooklands by Kay Petre. It was made as a pedal car but fitted with a two-speed moped engine by a local enthusiast and bought for the author's son Ross. Chris is shown here fettling it.

The 1920 single-geared Nortons, BS (Brooklands Special) and BRS (Brooklands Road Special) were tuned by the legendary 'Wizard' O'Donovan and sold with a certificate confirming that they had lapped Brooklands at 80mph.

A 1938 Triumph Speed Twin. Edward Turner's vertical twin revolutionised motorcycle design all over the world. All major motorcycle manufacturers had to follow Triumph with their own vertical twin designs.

Mid-1920s 250cc two-stroke Levis. It was a very popular runabout in its day, and in 1920 they achieved the first three places in the 250cc Lightweight TT.

A 1927 500cc Panther. The big Panthers always utilised the engine unit as a front-frame member.

DOT fitted all kinds of proprietary engines in the 1920s, but this machine has the unusual 350cc Bradshaw oil-cooled engine by the maverick designer, Granville Bradshaw. Its circulating oil system even cooled the cylinder barrel! This is believed to be a 1927 model, but the author had a 1923 model for many years.

The SOS was designed and manufactured by the fanatical motorcyclist Len Vale-Onslow, who still rode and worked on motorcycles until he was over 100 years old. The machine shown is a water-cooled two-fifty. Peter owned a 350cc version for many years.

One of the first overhead valve BSAs. This is a mid-1920s model similar to the one that was ridden by Chris's brother.

The 1928 Rudge ridden to victory in the 1928 Ulster Grand Prix by the great Graham Walker, father of Murray. It was the first bike to win a long-distance race at over 80mph.

The late 1930s BSAs were attractive machines and great fun to ride. Myself and 'T' rode many miles on them. This is a 500cc Empire Star, and the great Wal Handley lapped Brooklands on a highly tuned version, gaining a Brooklands Gold Star from which the first BSA Gold Star was developed.

A 1927 Derby-built McEvoy with 1,000cc JAP racing engine. Believed to be the machine successfully raced at Brooklands by George Patchett and, if so, later owned by the author but not with the original engine, which was sold by Stan Burnett for a fiver, if he was lucky. Note the Derby registration number.

Chris sitting on a 1931 ex-works Norton similar to the 1930 model he raced over half a century before.

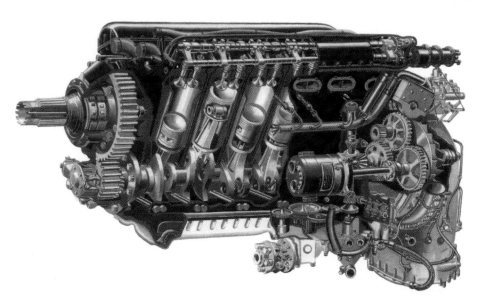

The Merlin is one of the most iconic aero-engines of all time, and the survival of England depended upon it in 1940 when it powered the Spitfires and Hurricanes in the Battle of Britain. It was a V-12 cylinder of 27 litres. Prototypes in February 1935 produced 950hp at the equivalent of 11,000ft. By 1940 on 100 octane fuel the Merlin Twos and Threes were producing 1,350hp. By the end of the war the latest marks were producing over 2,000hp.

A model of Chris's beloved *Katie*. Mosquito Mk VI P3 K.

A Mosquito in flight.

The American B24B Liberator. A powerful, well-armed, four-engined bomber.

A Messerschmitt ME 110 G-4. These deadly, radar-equipped night fighters wreaked havoc on the British bombers.

A Stearman biplane used for training at Miami, Oklahoma, and flown by Chris and Derek Sharpe.

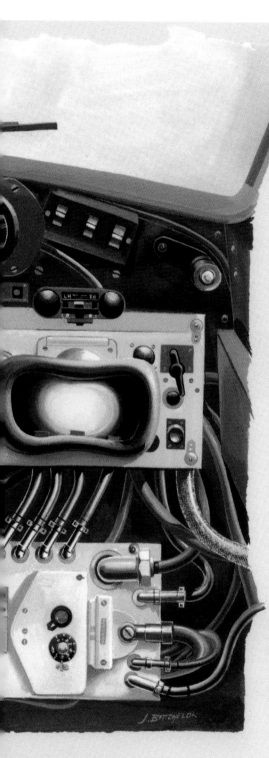

Mosquito NF.Mk.II/XII cockpit interior

It was April 1942 when the first Mosquito night-fighter squadron (No.157 Squadron, RAF) became operational. Fitted with AI (Airborne Interception) Mk.IV radar and ARI.5093 receiver, plus a formidable armament of four Hispano 20 mm cannons and four Browning 0.303 in machine guns, this fine combination in the NF.Mk.II proved to be very successful against enemy night intruders – indeed, all the night-fighter and night intruder Mosquitoes performed very well in their intended roles.

In the radar-equipped night-fighter Mosquitoes, the pilot and radar-operator sat side-by-side in the cramped cockpit. Initially, seating in the Mosquitoes was literally side-by-side, but a slight rearrangement later saw the seating staggered with the pilot in the left-hand seat being slightly further forward. The radar-operator guided the pilot onto the enemy aircraft using the Mosquito's on-board radar, usually until the pilot could see the target's exhaust flashes or the actual silhouette of the machine itself before making his attack. Mosquito cockpit interiors were fairly typical in their colouring for RAF aircraft of the period, with interior Grey-Green being the predominant colour for interior surfaces in most marks, together with black instrument panels and fittings such as the throttle quadrant. The crew seats were usually black or dark green.

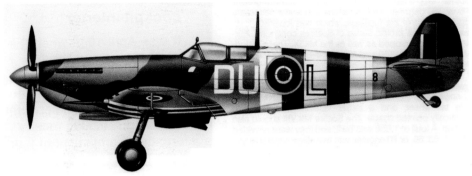

A Supermarine Spitfire Mk. IXC…

…and its formidable adversary, the Messerschmitt Bf 109.

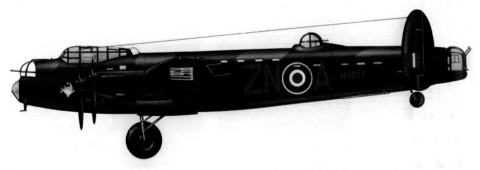

An Avro Lancaster Mk I, one of the bombers that bore the brunt of German night-fighter attacks.

Chris in an American ATA 6A (Harvard).

Once when flying in a Beaufort over the North Sea the instructor decided to return to base. Chris was somewhat bashful about pointing out to him that they were heading further out to sea rather than back home! Probably his years of experience monitoring a host of gauges on the Rolls-Royce test-beds helped him there!

The Beaufighter was made by the firm Bristol and was designed to take a Bristol radial engine, but due to enemy action it was decided to put the more readily available Merlins in their place. The Bristol was a left-hand tractor, whereas the Merlin was right-hand, and this meant that the slipstream from the propeller hit the tail fin on the wrong side. The fin was designed to take the Bristol prop wash, and with a Merlin engine the Beau II had a strong tendency to swing to the left on take-off requiring careful manipulation of the throttles and starboard brake application to keep the plane on the runway. Over the years Chris would land at different

Chris standing in front of a Fairchild PT 19A.

aerodromes to find battered hangars and other buildings to the left of the take-off runway and deduce that there had been Beau IIs at that station!

Pilots were, of course, supposed to practice single-engined flying, as they now had feathering pumps. He vividly remembers being briefed to climb to high altitude and feather one engine. Compared to other pupils, Chris was lucky in having run engines at Rolls-Royce with, first of all, fixed pitch then two position and finally feathering pumps, so he was quite familiar with the process. In the Beau cockpit at high altitude, however, it was a rather different matter. He gave the starboard feathering button a quick dab and the prop feathered. He then trimmed the aircraft straight and level. No one had said anything about turns etc, so straight-ahead he went and after some time decided to un-feather. His right hand was reluctant to leave the control column but, even so, he managed to give the un-feathering button a quick dab and out of the corner of his eye saw a

T.156/496
A Beaufighter Mk VI C.

A Junkers Ju 88G-I.

slight twitch of the blades which he wrongly interpreted as an indication that the battery was flat.

He continued straight-ahead for some time until his brain went into gear and he remembered that to un-feather you had to hold the button down. Controls were re-set and all was well, but later experience led him to believe that many pilots never got round to holding down that button.

Another part of the pilots' training was being put into an altitude chamber and having their oxygen supply turned off. There were four of them in the chamber, where they were told to write from one to 10 and repeat it ad infinitum. Watching the two fellows opposite he noticed that they had obviously passed out, but Chris thought he had managed not to; however, when he inspected his writing he noticed that he had gone 1,2,3,4 then squiggled all over the place before writing 8,9,10, so he realised that he, too, must have passed out at some point! It was a valuable lesson.

Chapter 20

THE 100 GROUP

In November 1943, 100 Group (Special Duties) of Bomber Command was established. The objective was to reduce the dreadful losses that night bombers were enduring over occupied Europe. Various squadrons and units had been fighting a secret war of electronics and radar, and the 100 Group brought them all together.

Air and ground radars, homing and jamming equipment, radio and navigational aids had all been pressed into service to destroy the German night fighters. The radar counter-measures operating from the ground were extended by two airborne systems: one was heavy bombers flying over occupied Europe with radio and radar jamming equipment, sometimes on 'spoofing' operations, and the other depended on the British night fighters. From June 1943 these night fighters had been engaged in high-level intruder operations against their German counterparts.

The 100 Group started with seven fighter squadrons, and after their tour of duty they would go for a 'rest' of six months as bomber support units, though they could still be called on to continue flying on combat operations if the testing of new equipment called for it.

But despite all the efforts of the brave men who flew through those deadly night skies, doing everything they possibly could to protect the bombers, the German night fighters continued to exact a murderous toll. When the bomber streams attacked German cities they presented easy targets for the radar-equipped enemy night fighters. They were as vulnerable as minnows in a tank with predatory pike.

On the night of 30–31 March 1944 there was a 795 bomber attack on Nuremburg in which 95 bombers were lost. Mosquito 100 Group pilot, pilot R.G. 'Tim' Goodman, actually saw 44 shot down.

Chris with his soulmate, his wife Madge.

Chapter 21

CHRIS MEETS MIKE ADAMS

At Charter Hall the trainee pilots were teamed up with their navigators, and Chris was allocated Sergeant Mike Adams. Mike was a rather quiet person so, at first, Chris found it difficult to get to know him, but what really mattered was how he would perform under combat conditions.

At the end of 1943 they were posted to Little Snoring, in Norfolk. The code-name was 'Notified by cable', but Chris's mother soon worked out that it was near Fakenham in Norfolk. Chris and Michael were now in 515 Squadron 100 Group, about to fly Mosquito Mark VI fighter-bombers armed with four 20mm cannon, four .303 machine guns and capable of carrying either a belly tank or two 500lb bombs. Their job was, as part of 100 Group,

Pilot Officer Chris on the left with his navigator Flight Sergeant Mike Adams.

to harass the German night-fighter bases in an attempt to reduce the dreadful toll that the RAF heavy bombers were experiencing.

Initially they flew a Beau II, and one day Chris reported a defect in one of the engines. The Flight Sergeant in charge of ground crew started to tell Chris that there was nothing wrong, but after Chris had talked to him and explained his reasons for reporting the fault he found that from then on the Flight Sergeant had instructed the other ground crew to be careful what they said to Chris about Merlins as he knew what he was talking about. At Little Snoring they were busy re-equipping with Mark VI Mosquitos and sometimes they would be delivered by an attractive young lady, who would climb out of the plane and then swiftly depart to carry out another delivery. Chris's Squadron Commander was 'Cordite' Lambert, so-called because of his frequent reference to the phrase 'Smell the cordite'. His Flight Commander was Squadron Leader Shaw, and Chris got on very well with him. Sadly, he went 'Missing in action' on D-Day.

If you have seen many films on flying in World War Two you will know that all the fighter pilots had fancy MG sports cars with gorgeous blonde barmaids

Chris conforms to fighter pilot stereotype in his Morgan Four-Four.

Another view of Chris's Four-Four. No branded petrol was available during the war, it was all 'Pool' petrol which, from memory, was about 75 octane. To eke out his petrol ration Chris would, on occasion, manage to scrounge a few gallons of 100 octane aviation fuel then persuade a friendly garage to let him have two or three gallons of paraffin, which although not rationed was in short supply. His Morgan would then run happily on a mixture of two gallons of pool, two gallons of paraffin and one gallon of aviation fuel.

in the passenger seats. Right? Wrong! Chris conformed to this stereotype with his Morgan Four-Four, but there was, believe it or not, only one other car in the squadron, though most of the aircrew were motorcyclists. The other car belonged to Squadron Leader Shaw's navigator, but far from being a sports car it was a little family saloon.

The aircrew were accommodated in Nissen huts situated around the aerodrome, and fortunately during the time that they were waiting for Mosquitos they lost no crews, so Chris got to know all the pilots and navigators.

As the new planes arrived Chris flew several of them and was delighted when PZ 217 P3-K was allotted to him. She was a good aeroplane, and Chris quickly got all controls synchronised, no doubt annoying his ground crew by asking them if they knew exactly how to make the adjustments required. Eventually realising that Chris knew exactly what he was talking about, however, they formed a very rewarding relationship. In fact, the widow of his engine mechanic still keeps in touch.

While the letter 'K' was usually reported as 'kilo' over radio communications, Chris decided instead to call his Mosquito 'Katie' and from then on always referred to her as 'My beloved Katie'. Cordite Lambert once flew Katie and said to Chris that she was the 'best aeroplane on the squadron,' before quickly adding 'next to mine, of course.'

As part of their training they flew low-level daylight cross-countries, and on one of these Chris arranged to include Rolls-Royce, Derby, in his flight. He well remembers flying up Nightingale Road just above the roof of the main offices, where he noticed a dummy gun with a wooden barrel on the roof. He then had to pull up quite sharply to go over the trees in Osmaston Park at the

W10 E. W. 'Bunny' Adams and Flight Sergeant Frank A. Widdecombe of 515 Squadron explain how they shot down a Junkers 88 over Bonn on the night of 24–25 February 1945.

This picture shows the Mosquito's armament in the nose and the door through which the crew entered.

top of Nightingale Road and turned left for Nottingham. As he did so the starboard engine went into coarse pitch so he had one engine running at a normal 2,400rpm and the other badly out of synchronisation at about 1,800rpm. Due to his test bed experience he knew that the engine was not unhappy at this, so he kept on flying.

The Nottingham barrage balloons were at a low level, so he was pleased when Nottingham was behind him and he was able to return to Little Snoring. He reported the problem after he had landed and was asked why he had not feathered the propeller of the lower speed engine. He replied that half an engine was better than no engine and this was accepted. After the war he met some of his old colleagues from Rolls-Royce, including his fellow racing motorcyclist Dennis Jones, who had been going to lunch in Nightingale Road at that time and had seen Chris as he flew over.

A strange story was that of bed number three in Chris's hut, allocated to a young Pilot Officer Navigator. He was a really decent chap who, said Chris,

The badge of 100 Group. A Gorgon's head, three-winged monsters of Greek mythology with snakes for hair, huge fangs and gigantic teeth. The malaysian motto was 'confound and destroy'.

Air Commodore E.B. Addison, who established 100 Group.

The American P-47D-II-RE Thunderbolt.

A Heinkel He 219 V16.

had probably never used a four-letter word or engaged in any of the boozing, womanising antics of his fellows. When they eventually got operational he was lost on his first mission, so he was yet another of the 'good guys' who, unfortunately, did not win. The replacement who was allocated the same bed only lasted two Ops, as did the next one, and no one else who ever slept in that bed ever completed three ops. Now, the young devil-may-care pilots and navigators in that squadron were not superstitious but, even so, no one else chose to sleep in bed number three!

Air-to-ground and air-to-air firing practice was constantly undertaken and the pilots would throw about two bob into the kitty so that the best shot would win about a pound. Their 100 rounds of 20mm cannon ammunition were coloured so that all rounds that hit the target could be identified. Chris enjoyed these unofficial contests and always seemed to win, until Bob Preston

A Focke-Wulf Fw 190A-4/R6.

who, post war, became I/C of all British Airways flights north of Manchester, said 'I'm not throwing in as we might as well give Chris the money.' One day Chris shot up the target drogue so badly that it was brought over to Little Snoring as an example. Chris kept it until he went to Australia.

Another target was a 9ft square suspended between two steel pipes. Chris managed to shoot it down, knocking down a steel pipe at the same time! Walking into the flight office after landing he was greeted by a torrent of abuse to the effect that he need not think he had done anything clever, many others there had hit the post and his was just the final shot that did the job! Chris made no reply, but on the next practise firing the target again fell down as Chris fired, and this time the Squadron Leader said not a word.

Chapter 22

COMBAT

Britsh bombers were being decimated by the German night fighters, so the Mosquito night-fighting squadrons had been formed to attack them and their airfields. Chris and his navigator, Mike, had finally completed their seemingly endless period of training and so were preparing to start their first combat mission.

As their take-off time was before the mess dinner time, Chris and Mike had eaten a meal served up by the mess WAAFs just before they walked across to board their Mosquito. During this walk Chris reflected on their chances. He had seen it all before on the cinema screens when the intrepid, handsome pilot, accompanied by his trusty navigator, headed out into the war-torn skies of occupied Europe and shot hell out of the German fighter planes. They inevitably returned unscathed, covered with glory and with their aircraft riddled with bullet holes. After all, the good guys always win. In real life, however, he knew that the good guys did not always win. Many good men had failed to return, and they would not be the last.

A quick visual check round the plane, then up the half dozen steps, head down, to crawl into the cockpit. Mike had handed him his parachute and dinghy pack, and when Chris was aboard he handed his safety equipment to him which he placed on Mike's seat. He then followed Chris in. When they were both seated they put on their parachute straps. Then came the 'HTMPFFG' checks – hatches and harness, trim and throttle, mixture and air intakes, pitch, fuel content, cocks, flaps, gills. They then put on their helmets, plugging them in to the intercom and radio. Next they fastened their face masks, because despite their 'below 2,000ft' operations they always used oxygen to improve night-vision. Then, with all checks completed, Chris glanced across at Mike. Mike had been allocated to Chris as his navigator, but he knew very little about him. Obviously he had completed his training satisfactorily but he seemed a very quiet chap with little to say. How would he perform under fire? Come to think of it, thought Chris, how will I perform under fire? They were both about to find out.

There was no more time for reflection; it was time to go. A few pumps of prime then the starter pressed and the twin Merlins burst into life. They were set to idle while Chris checked oil pressure, coolant temperature and all other instruments. Then the throttles opened to 2,000rpm for single ignition checks. Everything was in order, so Chris signalled 'chocs away' and taxied out of the dispersal area onto the perimeter track and to the down-wind end of the operational runway.

A final check and then a flash of light from the control tower; there was no radio as a security measure. Off with the navigation lights used during taxiing, throttles opened, brakes off, then the Mosquito started to roll down the runway. The Mossie was not a bad 'swinger', but the odd dab of brake could be used as speed increased, and usually you would not get to full power until the tail lifted at about 100mph.

Lift off. Revs 3,000rpm, boost 12 pounds per square inch, not the maximum 16psi only used in combat. All gauges recording the correct figures. It was a black night, so Chris was immediately flying on instruments, something that with his previous Merlin test-bed experience he probably found easier than most pilots. His experimental aero-engine test work had entailed the constant monitoring of over a dozen gauges so the Mosquito control panel, which, to the un-tutored eye, appears to be a bewildering jumble of gauges, was not at all complicated for Chris.

Revs were set to 2,400, boost only 4psi and they were on their way at 260mph. Chris had noticed that the latest Mosquitos had paddle blade propellers which were, no doubt, an advantage at high altitude but at low level reduced cruising speed to 250mph. As he had not been allocated a new plane, he was in a 'borrowed' Mossie with the early model propeller blades.

The few landmarks that they could pin-point on their way confirmed that Mike's calculations had been accurate, and they continued to be accurate right up to their target area. Chris's logbook records Brussels, Charleroi and strong light flak at Melbroeke, which was their first encounter with the very active aerodrome defences that they were destined to experience in the future. Chris's misgivings about Mike were now put behind him.

With the Mosquito illuminated at the apex of a cone of searchlights and the target of deadly fire, Mike never lost his cool watching the incoming tracers. Chris kept his eyes on the instruments while Mike shouted instructions: port, port, dive, then starboard, climb, dive again…His head must have been swivelling round as the flak was coming from all sides, though after what seemed like an age, but would probably only have been minutes, the Mosquito flew clear and unharmed.

Their patrol time over, they headed back to base, and during the journey Chris told Mike to keep awake at all costs and not to fall asleep as some navigators were reputed to do on the return back to the airfield. Mike was also told to give Chris thump if he appeared to become a bit sleepy over the North Sea.

The return flight, however, was uneventful, and they contacted the appropriate course station in good time so that their radar image could be identified as friendly. Eventually, over the UK coast, they changed to Base Frequency and advised them that 'Pale Green 21', Chris's code number, was coming home. It was a hazy night so Chris called for permission to join the circuit, where he followed the Drem system – lights on poles around the circuit. As he turned onto the base leg the illuminated letters LS confirmed that he was, indeed, at Little Snoring, and as he followed the Drem lights they led him into the approach, then the hooded runway lights came into view and he made a smooth touch-down.

When 23 Squadron joined them at Little Snoring after having been operating in North Africa, they laughed when they were told how difficult it was to be sure that you were at Little Snoring without the Drem system. Shortly afterwards one of their pilots was heard to call 'Turning off runway' when there was no sign of him. He had landed at another airfield a few miles away!

Next, Chris taxied to the dispersal area, where his ground crew were waiting for him to check for any damage and rectify any control problems that he might have experienced. Unlike some pilots, Chris knew exactly how to adjust throttle or pitch controls etc so that all levers would coincide in their positions during flight. He probably annoyed some of the crew by asking if they knew how to make such adjustments, let alone telling them how.

Then they went off to de-briefing, where Chris gave his best recollections of the flight: no, he could not confirm what damage, if any, he had inflicted, as he had been far too busy dodging the defenders' instant response to his cannon and machine gun fire at enemy airfields.

Thankfully, their night ended with a visit to the mess, where night duty WAAFs served a meal, and then finally to their billets, careful not to disturb the other crews who were sound asleep.

As Chris and Mike attempted to drift off to sleep they reflected that they were a combat crew at last and had lived to fight another day.

Chapter 23

FLYING OPS OVER OCCUPIED EUROPE

C hris's navigator Mike Adams was always careful to observe all instructions, and an example came on the first occasion that they loaded up with two 500lb bombs. Off they went across the Channel into occupied Europe, found an operational aerodrome, dived towards the runway, opened the bomb doors and then Chris signalled: 'Bombs away.' But where were they? After the expected five-second delay, there was no explosion! On their return to base the bomb doors were opened and there were the bombs. Why? It appeared that Mike had been told not to force any switch, but as they had never dropped any practice bombs he did not know that the arming switch had three positions: Off, Off and On. He had carefully put it into the first detent but, of course, this was still an 'Off' position.

With the armament officer aboard the plane, Chris checked that all was well by dropping the two fragmentation bombs onto a sandbank covered with seals. The idea was that the seals reduced the fish stocks, so killing them would help to preserve food. While the armament officer yapped on about how many seals he had killed, Chris refrained from looking at the poor creatures!

Among the many enemy aerodromes they attacked was one called Gilzerijen, and due to the fact that they lost several crews there they called it 'Gilzy the Chopper'. One night, when returning from North Germany, Chris was flying over northern Holland when he saw what he thought was some fool taking off from a Dutch-based aerodrome with his tail light on.

A Mk VI FB Mosquito in flight.

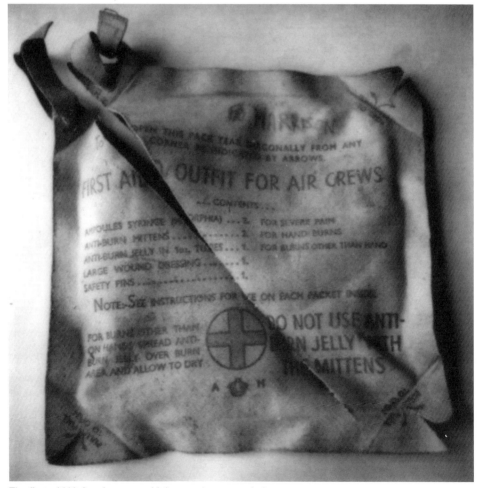

The first-aid kit for aircrews, which was always carried.

Chris quickly turned towards him and at the same time opened up to combat power but was amazed to see the enemy plane climb rapidly away from him. He then realised it was a jet propelled ME169 which had recently come into service.

On another flight, returning from the Continent, he was advised that Little Snoring was closed due to fog, and he was vectored north towards Foulsham which was equipped with Fido. As he approached the aerodrome the fog ahead gradually lit up into brilliant red, and by the time he was into the circuit it was very bright, but there was still no sign of the runway. He was vectored round again and on the approach he was told to reduce height. Suddenly he

An 'escape photograph', which was part of the escape kit. The French could forge other documents in the event of aircrew being shot down, but not photographs.

Wing Commander Freddie 'Cordite' Lambert (left), CO of 515 Squadron, and Squadron Leader Harold 'Mick' Martin of Dambusters fame. He was supposed to be 'resting' at Little Snoring but flew many Ops.

burst into a blazing red tunnel of light with 50-gallon drums of burning kerosene spaced along the edges of the runway. He landed safely and was instructed where to turn off, and when he and Mike disembarked there was a WAAF driver waiting to drive them back to Little Snoring. Next morning they were driven back to Foulsham to collect *Katie*.

Chris and Mike encountered all kinds of hazards when flying over occupied Europe. On one occasion they were even attacked by a train! They were flying quite low over the North German plain, and many of the trains used in that area were well armed and quite capable of defending themselves. Fortunately no bullets or cannon-fire hit them.

On another night, when they were just about to cross the enemy coast, up came a hail of flak which they managed to avoid. Once in the clear, Mike said 'I saw that ship, but I felt sure that it was one of ours!'

If they found an operational enemy aerodrome they would patrol it in the hope of catching a returning night fighter. Unfortunately, however, it was only on their final approach that they showed a small white light on their nose and you had to be on the far side of the aerodrome to see it. Even if you were fortunate enough to see the light you would be too far away to engage the enemy plane. By the time they did get to the approach side of the aerodrome the lights were switched off so you could no longer locate it. In addition to that, there were always plenty of gun positions on the approach, so they would encounter a murderous hail of flak.

When attacking planes on their runways, he was often given a fright by having to evade his own bullets as well of those of the German defences. The mixture of ball, high explosive, armour piercing and incendiary would ricochet when hitting the ground and, although the incendiaries were visible, many of the other bullets were not, so avoiding them was an additional hazard.

Occasionally they engaged in daylight operations when they attacked 'Targets of opportunity' such as trains, barges, road transport etc. On such operations they flew in pairs, but once when his beloved *Katie* was being serviced he flew another plane, and finding that the undercarriage would not indicate 'Up and locked' he returned to Little Snoring. They always kept radio

The bar at Little Snoring. Above the bar hung a scrubbing brush counterbalanced by a dice. When Ops for 515 or 23 Squadrons were cancelled, i.e. 'scrubbed', the scrubbing brush was lowered. When they were on Ops the dice was lowered as they were 'dicing', a term which came from 'Speed demons dicing with death', coined to describe motorcyclists hurtling round Brooklands in its early days.

silence on operations, so he had to land to explain his return. While he was explaining the problem to the ground crew, however, Cordite Lambert drove up, jumped out of his vehicle and rushed across shouting 'What's the matter, are you yellow?' To this Chris instantly replied that he should stop talking like a ★★★ and get him another aeroplane! Cordite, however, was to get his revenge!

One night Chris and Mike flew over what appeared to be a prison camp, and as they approached the far side Chris gave the guard post a good burst. Although it was night the camp, for some reason, was lit up. The Germans had Radar, but it was inferior to the British system at that time. It was in the form of a beam and as it passed across you it became audible as a low pitched buzz. Sometimes it would cut out, then re-focus and follow you, but by flying low you were usually able to lose it.

At de-briefing one night Chris was reprimanded for engaging in 'dangerous conduct while over enemy territory'. Little Snoring was about 120ft above sea level and the North German plain only about 20ft. After attacking a ground target he reported that his altimeter, set to zero at Little Snoring, recorded below zero when over the target. Naughty boy!

On one early operation, as they crossed the North Sea, they were amazed to see an enormous number of planes, some with lights on, all flying eastwards, and the next day they found that it was an early 1,000 bomber raid. They very seldom saw bomber operations but one night in North Germany, with no activity in the area, they suddenly saw the sky to their south illuminated by thousands of white flares, followed shortly afterwards by coloured flares then a voice, unusually on their frequency, calling for 'Back-up on blue'. This was obviously a pathfinder operation and the 'Master' had an Australian accent. Of course, the explosives and incendiaries followed, but they were too far away to see any results.

Their daylight operations included close-cover escort duties with the Lancaster bombers when they attacked the La Rochelle U-boat pens. Many brave men died on these operations with no chance whatsoever of even scratching the paint on a U-boat. They were protected by a huge thickness of concrete and were completely impregnable. To reach La Rochelle, they had to fly over the Brittany Peninsular and run the gauntlet of German anti-aircraft fire, only to endure it again on their return journey. Many years later on holiday in Brittany we would see these long-disused anti-aircraft sites on the coast and remember the brave aircrew who flew over them.

On these operations the Mosquitos carried fuel drop tanks. Once when crossing the Channel, Chris realised that the fuel in his starboard drop tank would not transfer, so the fuel in it could not be used. He decided that he would dump it and its 50 gallon contents in the sea. He had no idea, however, of how much this would alter the trim, so coordinating with Mike he firmly held the controls until Mike was prepared to turn the trim handle in the right direction. When it was approximately right Chris made the final adjustments.

Returning from one of these operations and landing in south-west England there were calls for his plane, which had just landed, to keep rolling as the next plane which was dangerously low on fuel was right behind him on the approach. Fortunately, however, it landed safely and all was well.

It occurred to someone that it might be a good idea if the Mosquito pilots could know how a Spitfire or Me109 could manoeuvre as compared to their machines, and so a Spitfire pilot came along to tell them the bad news. After his talk the pilot asked Chris if he would like to do a circuit in the Spitfire but Chris, much to his later regret, refused the offer thinking that he could pull it in some other time, though of course the chance never arrived again.

One night, when he was deep in Germany, he was patrolling over an enemy aerodrome where there were signs of activity, hoping to intercept a returning night fighter, and stayed there far too long after he should have returned to base. It was custom to change over to base frequency as they crossed the North Sea and normally if anyone was more than 10 minutes late it meant that they were not coming back. Apparently Chris had already been put into that category, but as he changed to base frequency he heard someone call so he just pressed the transmit button and asked 'Why?' He was later told that one of the Flying Control WAAFs immediately announced on hearing Chris's call that he was safely on the way home. He never did find out who she was.

'Bombing up' a Mosquito at Little Snoring.

Of course, these pilots had to spend quite a bit of time in the Link Trainer. In this device you sat in a small box rigged out like a cockpit with a lid on. The instructor could communicate with you and tell you to perform various manoeuvres, and a mechanical device on his table printed out all your turns etc. More complicated were written instructions which, when performed correctly, would print out the raised fore-finger, folded fingers and thumb of a right hand. One day the instructor was so pleased with Chris's effort that he inked in fingernails and added a few extra bits, then endorsed it: 'With the compliments of the Link Department'. Chris promptly folded the still wet, inked paper into his pocket and still has it to this day!

Soon after mid-1944 they lost another Flight Commander, and he was replaced by the newly promoted Squadron Leader Mick Martin of Dambuster fame. Chris well remembers that on his arrival Mick was a Flight Lieutenant on one shoulder of his battledress and a Squadron leader on the other! He always got on very well with Mick, and one day he asked Chris to visit a bomber base and pick up a terrier puppy called Joe. Poor little Joe was as deaf as a post when he landed, but this soon cleared up.

ENSA concert parties used to visit the base, and their light-hearted shows were always welcome. Once Chris was in the officers' mess for a pre-op takeoff meal which was empty apart from the ENSA people who had already performed. As Chris sat there Joe trotted out of the mess kitchen where the WAAFs looked after him. One of the young ladies who had, no doubt, been kicking her heels up on stage spotted Joe and called out 'Look at this dahling little puppy'. At this Joe looked round, decided all was well, squatted down and made a large deposit. An embarrassed WAAF ran out from the kitchen with the necessary equipment and sorted things out, but Chris was sure she felt nowhere near as embarrassed as the 'dahling puppy' dancer!

One night Chris and Mike were 'on the programme' – due to fly on operations that night. When they turned up for briefing they were met by a corporal at the door and told that they were not on the programme after all. So they would survive for another night! They later found out that everyone on that operation was decorated and that his beloved *Katie* had been flown by

Chris's beloved *Katie*. She sleeps at the bottom of the North Sea.

Cordite Lambert. So Cordite had his revenge! It was a disappointment for Chris, but he shrugged his shoulders and accepted it. He was, however, very disappointed that Mike Adams missed out on a decoration, especially as he had flown a few operations with Cordite. About 20 years ago Chris wrote to Cordite and asked him what his recollections were of the medal-winning night. The reply he received either indicated that Cordite was ageing rapidly or that he had dodged the question. Chris never found out about the mission.

Chapter 24

AIR–SEA RESCUE

Early on Chris had been appointed the Air Sea Rescue Officer for 515 Squadron and had successfully passed a course to qualify for this at Blackpool. There was, however, only one occasion when those skills were put to use. One of the squadron's Mosquitos crossed the Dutch coast en route for home with an engine on fire. The navigator baled out close to Holland but the pilot hung on until his burning engine could be seen from the English coast and then he, too, baled out and was quickly picked up.

Advised of the navigator's plight, Chris and Mike headed off accompanied by Flight Lieutenant Josh Hoskins and his navigator, 'Jonah' Jones, and they began a search off the Dutch coast. The sea was choppy, making it very difficult to see a dinghy in those conditions, but when they were about to give up, Jonah spotted it. Even after Chris circled, following Jonah, it was some minutes before he could distinguish the dinghy so he then flew to the coast and checked time and distance course to fly from a landmark to Josh's orbit and then set off for home.

Chris arranged for a Walrus seaplane to pick up the dinghy, but in case the sea was too rough for a Walrus to land he also organised a backup launch. Chris and Josh took off again but, once again, they could not spot the dinghy. They were beginning to assume that the Germans had already picked it up when fortune smiled and Josh spotted it again some miles from where they had originally found it, and they circled round it once again.

After some time they were all startled to see what they thought was an ME109 swooping down out of the cloud cover some miles north of them but, to their relief, they realised it was a Mustang which was being followed by the Walrus. Before attempting to land, the Walrus dropped a flare, which was a great help in keeping the dinghy in sight, but when it did go in to land

A Supermarine Walrus which did sterling service in Air-Sea rescues during the war.

Chris was alarmed to see it disappear in a cloud of spray! Fortunately it re-appeared, taxied to the dinghy, picked up the navigator, fired a few rounds into the dinghy and made several attempts to take off because the wing floats repeatedly dug in, slewing it off course. Finally, however, it managed to take off successfully. It was not a moment too soon, reflected Chris, as he was exhausted from his pointless mental efforts attempting to lift the Walrus off the sea!

Chris decided to head for home, leaving the Walrus to amble along accompanied by the Polish Mustangs, at which point he saw the backup rescue launch heading east. They flew over it, waving their hands to try to tell them they must turn back, but without success, so then Josh climbed until he was in radio contact with the UK who could then advise the launch to turn back.

Chapter 25

FINAL DAYS OF COMBAT

One night, returning from deep in France and approaching Brussels, Chris and Matt were amazed to see a convoy of road transport heading west with full headlights on. Naturally Chris turned and attacked it, opening fire at maximum range. This, however, was a mistake as the moment Chris's cannon started to flash the lights were extinguished and Chris could no longer see either road or the transport. He did not claim any strikes but he was sure that the occupants would have had a severe fright. Chris simply reported it as something unusual. Within a few days, however, news of the failed Hitler assassination attempt came to light, together with the rapid departure of Rommel for the Western front. Chris considers that it was very likely that he had attacked the Rommel transport.

At Little Snoring they had an American captain who flew Lockheed Lightnings and two lieutenants who flew Mustangs on night operations. Chris never found out exactly what they did, but he did see that they had a Jeep.

The American Mustang, a great all-round fighter powered by the Rolls-Royce Merlin engine.

Apparently the captain wanted to fly a Mosquito, so Chris was instructed to get in touch with him to let him fly *Katie*. It never occurred to Chris to suggest that he should fly the American's Lightning as it was just another aeroplane, but only the Americans had Jeeps, so he was allowed to drive it and thoroughly enjoyed hammering it over all the rough terrain he could find, so he felt that he had got the better part of the bargain!

The jet-propelled Messerschmitt Me 262A-2a Sturmvogel.

The jet-propelled Meteor.

A little while later, a jet Meteor instructor wanted to fly a Mosquito, so Chris was briefed to visit the Meteor base to allow him to do so. He arrived at mid-afternoon and suggested that he would like to fly a Meteor in exchange and so, after an earlier-than-usual meal, he retired to his bunk and studied the pilot's notes for flying the new machine.

At breakfast he talked things over with the Meteor instructor and asked lots of questions, but the instructor said that it looked as if Chris knew even more about the plane than he did. They then went over to a parked Meteor where Chris asked even more questions and was told to beware of dirt from the cockpit floor if he attempted any aerobatics. Chris then watched some of the conversion course pilots attempting to try the Meteor's unfamiliar three-point tricycle undercarriage and then he took off, heading straight to Derby! The Meteor had barely an hour's endurance, so Chris did a quick beat up over the Rolls-Royce Sinfin site and then turned back for base. Flying control, no doubt expecting that he would be somewhere close to the aerodrome, called to enquire about his position, and he replied, somewhat cryptically, 'I's a-coming home' and some minutes later he made a good landing back at base.

In the autumn of 1944 Chris had a weekend off so he decided to fly the squadron's twin-engined Airspeed Oxford to Castle Donington aerodrome which, after having been used as a training centre, had been closed down. His parents lived at Castle Donington, so having landed at the completely deserted

The Halifax bomber.

The Wellington bomber.

base he taxied to a hedge where he knew he could climb over onto a lane that led to the main road through the village. After the weekend he walked back up the hill, climbed through the hedge again and, after firing up the Oxford, returned to Little Snoring. Nowadays this aerodrome is the busy East Midlands airport.

Post-war records show that in the 12 months that they were operating at Little Snoring the squadron chalked up 43 lost aircraft. They would regularly hear the BBC say that 'Last night Mosquitos of Bomber Command attacked Berlin and all aircraft returned safely'. There was never a word about the 'secret' night-fighter Mosquitos that were being lost on a tragically regular basis.

Chapter 26

INSTRUCTING ON WELLINGTONS

When Chris's tour of operations was completed he thoroughly enjoyed his week's leave, during which he managed to get a hard-to-come-by roll of film, so he headed back to Little Snoring to get a photograph of *Katie*. When he got there, however, he found that she was gone. Where was she? Apparently in the North Sea! Returning from an operation, Little Snoring had been closed due to fog so she was vectored south to a clear aerodrome but had just disappeared en route.

Many years later Tom Cushing, whose family owns the Little Snoring aerodrome, wrote to Chris to say that he had a surprise for him. After Chris's last operational flight he told fellow pilot Terry Groves that as his plane was due for servicing he could borrow *Katie* for a daylight operation. Terry refuelled it in France then took off and strafed an enemy airfield full of parked aeroplanes, with ground fire returned from only a few defensive machine guns; however, while he was parked at the French aerodrome someone had taken a photograph of *Katie* so eventually Chris got her picture!

Chris was next posted to Cranfield where, rather than instruct on Mosquitos, he opted to fly 'classroom' Wellingtons. These had Mk10 Radar in the nose and four Radar sets in the cabin, where an instructor supervised four pupils who did their best to chase the Hurricanes that were used as targets. His instruction on the Wellington consisted of 30 minutes as a passenger as they were not dual equipped! He was then sent off for preliminary experience. By coincidence, the day he was sent off was the day after the enormous underground bomb dump explosion at Fauld near Burton upon Trent. He headed there and spent some time circling the incredible area of damage that this 4,000-ton explosion had caused. While circling he only saw one other plane in the vicinity. On returning to Cranfield, he landed on a runway that had an orchard just before the approach.

'New boy' Christopher, however, used to the Mosquito and forgetting that there were several feet of Wellington below his seat, scraped the tops of the fruit trees and was ordered to 'Report to flying control'. There was no damage to the plane, but the lady who owned the orchard complained about 'drunken pilots' causing problems. 'No', says Chris 'I was quite sober, just stupid!'

When flying with various instructor navigators, Chris would occasionally do some single-engined flying while waiting for the target plane to get into their area. Invariably the ex-operational navigator would come into the cockpit to ask what the problem was and usually, being told that Chris was just practising, he would say that his pilots always said that there was plenty of time to do that when the need arose.

Chris reflected on his first single-engined flight and, while he understood the reasoning, experience told him that it was mistaken. He well remembered seeing a Wellington which happened to be near his base at the time, coming in on one engine far too fast, overshooting and wrecking the plane but, fortunately, with no loss of life. On another occasion he was in the control tower and saw a Mosquito coming into land far too fast on one engine. Chris told the flight controller to tell the pilot to retract his undercarriage to slow the plane down as he sped halfway down the runway on his main wheels. The pilot failed to do so and the plane ran off the end of the runway, hit a hedge and flipped onto its back. Chris had his bicycle handy so he rushed to the site where the pilot had just managed to get out of the plane, but the navigator was still strapped in. Chris immediately attempted to release him, a six footer nicknamed Lofty. As he was twitching Chris assumed that he was still alive, but when he finally got him out the doctor, who had just arrived, pronounced him dead with a broken neck. He then asked the pilot why he had not retracted his undercarriage, to which the reply was that he was too tightly strapped in. I will not quote Chris's answer to that, but suffice it to say that it was far from polite!

One day an attractive lady reporter came along to have a look at the Mosquitos and Chris, who had been promoted to Flight Lieutenant, was told to take care of her. They went to dispersal and Chris showed her all round the machine. She then wanted to climb the 6ft ladder and get into the cockpit, asking Chris if he would assist her to do so. Chris explained that as she only had a short skirt she would have to go on her knees, face well down, to get into the cockpit, but she insisted. Chris said 'All I can record is that they were very neat and immaculate!' Her write-up mentioned a quite co-operative Christopher!

About this time he was posted to Cranwell, and instead of instructing pupils he flew numerous boffins to demonstrate how Mk10 Radar worked. Chris was also sent on several fatal accident investigations. On one of these a Mosquito, apparently on fire, had hit the ground where there was barely 2ft of topsoil. The farmer and his wife told him that they were awakened by a loud engine noise and had seen a red glow in the air from the burning plane as it passed their window. They then heard the crash. The farmer had rushed out to see if there were any survivors, but there was no chance. Chris had never seen such a wreck, as even the engine crankshafts were in little pieces. In accordance with custom, two blankets were laid out and any small bits of flesh and bone were shared between the two, differentiating light hair from black or anything that could distinguish one from the other, but there was a negligible amount of remains.

The procedure was to load the coffins with sand up to normal body weight and mark them 'Not to be opened'. Sometimes grieving relatives would ignore this and, understandably, would complain about what they found.

After the official clear-up the farmer told Chris that he had found an elbow joint which he had buried under a hedge. Chris thanked him for what he considered to be the best possible action, as far more of that body remained at the scene rather than in the coffin.

While Chris normally flew Wellingtons, on one occasion the unit was posted to an aerodrome quite some distance away, and as the Hurricane pilots were not the best at cross-country flying he decided that he would lead them in formation to the new aerodrome. This went very well until there was cloud ahead and, as usual, Chris just flew straight through it. All of a sudden he heard the thunder of a Merlin engine just over his head and then heard the throttle slam shut. His fellow pilot had attempted to keep close to Chris's plane, only to lose sight of him and then realise he was going too fast. Fortunately a collision was avoided, but it was a close-run thing. Once through the cloud, they all re-assembled and proceeded to their new base with no more problems.

At Christmas 1944 Chris called in at Little Snoring and went up to his old Nissan Hut to see who he remembered. After chatting away one of the airman asked Chris if he had noticed the bed. There, where number three bed had been, was an open space! It appeared that the jinx on bed number three had never lifted, and as everyone knew that 'no one who slept in that bed had ever survived for three Operations', the bed had finally been removed.

A Mk X Airbourne Radar Classroom inside a Wellington Bomber.

After the war and back at Rolls-Royce, Chris found that at Burnaston aerodrome near Derby there was an RAFVR centre where Wing Commander Roxborough was in charge, so he signed up and learnt to fly a Tiger Moth. One of his fellow pilots was Alan Bramson who, as an aviation reporter, had flown over 200 different types of aircraft and had written about them in aviation journals. They became good friends.

Chapter 27

AFTER THE WAR

When Chris and Madge first went to Australia it was an exciting time as they were starting a new life in a new country. They immediately liked the Australians, who made the newly arrived Poms most welcome. They loved the climate and had no regrets about leaving the English winters behind.

Chris meets Formula One Champion Jackie Stewart.

On the work front it was all go for Chris, and that is the way he liked it. A new Rolls-Royce factory was being built to handle the servicing and repair of the Civil Viscount Darts, together with Dart and Avon turbo-jets used by the Royal Australian Air Force. A new Test House was being constructed and all equipment installed. Chris would be in charge, using Dart test equipment he had invented and which came into service all over the world. When work started Chris was in his element with a heavy workload and, as always, no shortage of problems to solve. Some of them even baffled head office at Derby, but Chris found the solutions.

Chris had known Harvey-Bailey for years in Derby, and they had always got on well together. This continued in Australia for a while but, after a time, Harvey-Bailey's attitude started to change. It was almost imperceptibly at first, with innuendo depreciating Chris at staff meetings. Finally Harvey-Bailey was able to manoeuvre Chris into a difficult position and dismiss him, leaving him out on his own and out of the firm that had been his life.

Chris's Avon/Dart engine test crew.

The first TAA Viscount.

With Jim Searle, Philippines Airlines.

The next few years were very difficult indeed for Chris as his relationship with Harvey-Bailey became an issue when applying for other jobs. Eventually he got a job with the aviation tyre division at Goodyear and, once again, was able to get on with the task which he had always enjoyed: problem solving.

A surprise find in Goroka, New Guinea.

One of the numerous World War Two aircraft wrecks in New Guinea.

Chris introduced a B747 brake modification, which Akron insisted was a Qantas problem, but airlines all over the world took it up. The same occurred with tyres. Multiple re-treading is standard aviation procedure, but Chris's 'no cost' innovation increased tyre multiple re-tread reliability. This system was also adopted worldwide.

Chapter 28

CIVIL FLYING IN AUSTRALIA

When Chris came to Australia in 1954 he qualified for a commercial license with instrument and instructors' ratings. He then enjoyed weekend honorary instructing at the local Royal Aero Club.

At least one of his pupils became a 747 pilot at Qantas. He was once instructing another pupil when, after having shown her all the cockpit features, he wanted to reassure her and said 'Don't worry, it's just like a motor car, and when you have been in it a few times you will know where everything is.' To which she replied 'I'm not old enough to drive a motor car!'

Chris finished up having flown 39 types of aircraft – but to his regret he never flew a Spitfire!

THE BRITISH PEOPLE HAD THE LION'S HEART.
I HAD THE LUCK TO GIVE THE ROAR.

Winston Churchill